WHERE DO YOU? GET YOUR IDEAS ?

A WRITER'S GUIDE TO TRANSFORMING NOTIONS INTO NARRATIVES

WD

WRITER'S DIGEST
BOOKS

WritersDigest.com
Cincinnati, Ohio

Fred White

Special markets edition ISBN: 978-1-4403-4875-4

16 15 14 13 12 5 4 3 2 1

Edited by Scott Francis and Roseann Biederman
Designed by Claudean Wheeler
Cover illustrations by Anja Kaiser/Fotolia.com, Mark Markau/Fotolia.com, Alexandr Sidorov/Fotolia.com
Production coordinated by Debbie Thomas

DEDICATION

THIS TOO FOR YOU,
THERESE,
WITH LOVE

Love prays. It makes covenants with Eternal Power. —EMERSON

ACKNOWLEDGMENTS

I wish to express my gratitude to the superb editorial team at Writer's Digest Books, especially to Scott Francis, Roseann Biederman, and Claudean Wheeler.

Many thanks also to Jon Sternfeld, formerly with the Irene Goodman Literary Agency, for his early guidance and enthusiasm for my project.

And to my wife, Therese Weyna: Thank you for your shrewd suggestions, your continual encouragement, and your inspiration.

Contents

PART I: STRATEGIES

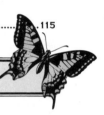

PART 2: APPLICATIONS

PART 1

Strategies

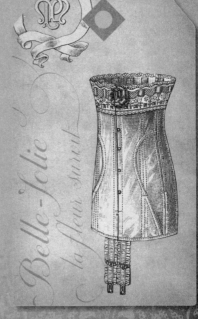

CHAPTER 1

Introduction

It's surprising how far an image can lead. —JAMES MERRILL

Nonwriters, understandably mystified by the creative process, frequently ask successful writers, "Where do you get your ideas?" On the surface the question seems illogical, naïve; not surprisingly, many writers do not take it seriously. Science fiction writer Harlan Ellison, for example, famously replied, "From Schenectady."

I, however, do not consider the question naïve. Maybe it has something to do with the fact that I myself have always been mystified by the creative process, the act of creating powerful works of art out of words (or brushstrokes or musical notation). I've devoured studies of creativity, such as Sigmund Freud's *On Creativity and the Unconscious*, Arthur Koestler's *The Act of Creation*, Jerome Bruner's *On Knowing: Essays for the Left Hand*, Brewster Ghiselin's anthology of essays, *The Creative Process*, Eric Maisel's *Creativity for Life*, and most recently, Jonah Lehrer's *Imagine: How Creativity Works*. Indeed there is an element of mystery to how a writer manages to create stories—and that's a good thing. When

I think about how I came to write my own short stories (two of which I'll be discussing in later chapters), I can fairly well explain the origins of this or that incident in my actual experience; but there always comes a point at which any attempt to explain the creative process falters—not surprising when you consider the astonishing complexity of the human brain and the numerous kinds of creativity that exist: One can place the word *creative* in front of virtually any activity, and it will make perfectly good sense—from creative financing to creative engineering to creative cooking. In fact, one could reasonably argue that if creativity were to vanish, civilization would stagnate.

The point that I want to stress, however, is that there is more practicality than mystery to the creative process. To approach anything creatively is to imbue it with new life, new possibility. But how, you may ask, does one do that? My answer: by approaching the activity with enthusiasm and a sense of purpose ("I so love to entertain children with stories that I am going to try as hard as I can to come up with story situations that will keep my child audience enthralled.") As Eric Maisel explains in *Creativity for Life*, "People are creative when they love what they are doing, know what they are doing, and actively engage in art-making."

THE AIM OF THIS BOOK

Where Do You Get Your Ideas? examines the processes of not only getting ideas but also *working* with them in order to transform them into stories—and by *stories* I mean narrative fiction or nonfiction. While it is true that there will always be an impenetrable veil of mystery behind some aspects of the creative process, there is nothing mysterious in learning to get ideas and turn them into publishable works.

Let's begin by carefully defining the phrase in question: What, exactly, is meant by "getting ideas?" The way in which the question is worded poses a problem. Are ideas literally *gotten* from somewhere, like apples plucked from a tree (or, for that matter, ordered from Schenectady)? Not quite! People tend to reduce a complex question to a simple one to make it more understandable, even at the cost of accuracy. In the case of "Where do you get your ideas?" I detect three underlying questions:

1. How do you recognize an idea with story potential?
2. How do you generate ideas "out of the blue"?
3. What steps do you take to develop your story out of the initial idea?

We will be looking closely at each of these more focused questions in order to arrive at a method of idea harvesting; but first we need to make sure what we mean by an *idea*. The *Random House Webster's Dictionary* offers eleven definitions, the first (and most basic) definition being, "Any conception existing in the mind as a result of mental understanding, awareness, or activity"; a second definition (more in keeping with our purposes here), "a plan of action; intention; a concept developed by the mind." To put it even more simply, an idea is a concept that is rooted (or made more meaningful) through understanding and experience.

Let's see how that works by considering the concept of *light*. Jot down whatever leaps to mind when you think of light. Embedded in that concept, like so many Chinese boxes, are experiences you have had with light in its many manifestations: sunlight, starlight, moonlight, candlelight. Plus there are the metaphoric extensions of light: divine light, an illuminating explanation, a sudden *bright* idea (think of the light bulb that flashes over the heads of cartoon characters). These metaphoric concepts are all derivatives of the root concept of light. Candles are derived from the idea of triumphing over darkness (or, in our time, from the idea of establishing a certain mood, say that of romance, or of spiritual contemplation. Another set of Chinese boxes will contain potential story premises: Candlelight, for example, can suggest a séance, which in turn can suggest a story premise about a woman who is desperately searching for a way to conjure up her dead husband's spirit because of a vital secret that must be revealed.

For the science fiction/fantasy novelist and essayist Ursula Le Guin, writers refer to having ideas as shorthand "to stand for the complicated, obscure, un-understood process of the conception and formation of what is going to be a story when it gets written down"—a process, Le Guin goes on to explain, that "may not involve ideas in the sense of intelligible thoughts . . . It may be a matter of mood, resonances, mental glimpses, voices, emotions, visions, dreams, anything."[1]

Everyone has ideas, of course, so why the mystery when it comes to ideas represented by creative works? At the risk of overgeneralizing, I would say that nonwriters, perplexed by how writers come up with imaginative story ideas, or assimilate the cauldron of ingredients that comprise one's life experiences into story content, have not yet discovered—or have not paid much attention to—their own powers of imagination, their own innate ability to take even a trivial act, say children entering a wardrobe closet, and then having that closet turn out to be a portal to a fantasy world. Where did C.S. Lewis "get" that idea for his Narnia novels? He got it by connecting an ordinary site (a walk-in closet) to an extraordinary one (a fantasy world). What motivated him to make such a strange connection? We can only conjecture. Perhaps it had something to do with his lifelong quest for the transcendent, for thinking about the ways in which ordinary events can lead us to extraordinary ones. In Chapter 3 we will look at different ways of conjuring up ideas for stories. But first things first: Let's take a closer look at the three cognitive processes I've identified in the blanket phrase, "getting an idea."

RECOGNIZING IDEAS WITH STORY POTENTIAL

You've heard it a thousand times: Story ideas are all around you! Yes, but that realization is not very helpful if you don't know how to spot "story potential." And before you can do that, you need to understand what is *meant* by story potential.

Let's say you and your spouse had partied a little too hearty and woke up the next morning in a not-quite-familiar room. "Honey, where are we?" was the first question that popped into your pounding head. Story potential? Oh yes. If you're Earl Hamner, Jr., you once fashioned that little nugget into one of the strangest of the original *Twilight Zone* episodes, "Stopover in a Quiet Town." You would have had the couple awaken to discover, little by little, that everything around them was fake—everything—from the stage-prop food in the fridge to the squirrel in the tree to the tree itself and even the grass—all the while wondering where the occasional giggle of a child was coming from. Where did Hamner "get that weird idea"? I suspect that he first spliced one ordinary idea—stopping off in a small town—to another ordinary idea, a man waking up with a hangover and asking his wife, "Honey, where are we?"—and then allowed his imagination to have free reign by way of several provocative "what if" questions:

- *What if* the couple had so much to drink the night before that they had no recollection of driving home?
- *What if* they were brought to a strange town instead of having driven there? What if aliens from another world had brought them?
- *What if* those aliens regarded the couple as pets from Earth and they gave those "pets" to their four-year-old daughter to add to her toy village?

"What if" questions, or variations thereof (What happens next? What are the consequences of X? and so on), are standard acts of cognition for all fiction writers.

GENERATING IDEAS OUT OF THE BLUE

Is it really possible to get ideas out of the blue; that is, through pure invention, without any particular thought or incident triggering the idea? Maybe not in any absolute sense; but relatively speaking, we get ideas out of the blue all the time without even trying. You're in the middle of planting roses, for example, and for no apparent reason you get a flash image of yourself uncovering the fossil skull of a creature that bears no resemblance to any known species on earth. *Now where did that idea come from*? you wonder. Your thoughts were entirely focused on roses! Well, it could have come from simply digging in the ground: It's rather easy to associate the digging with archaeology or paleontology. Or maybe you'd recently read a newspaper article about a new species of hominid that had been discovered in East Africa. Or maybe, as you were digging, you began wondering about the possibility of uncovering buried treasure. Our brains are wired for such associations; we are constantly forging new links among the multitude of experiences that make up our daily lives. Professional writers know that and cultivate the habit of making connections like that all the time, and make good use of what rhetoricians refer to as heuristic devices—playful activities that help you generate story or essay content—such as listing, mapping, character profiling, and creating collages or scrapbooks.

A word about the latter activity: It is often liberating to go beyond language in order to create collages that depict settings, characters, and situations for possible stories. A basic benefit of scrapbooking is that it can help you to acquire keen visual representations of the stories you want to tell. Are you getting ready to write a story about an Amish farming family? Then create collages that depict Amish farms, farming equipment, barn and farmhouse interiors, Amish clothing, foods (with recipes), and recreational activities. Mix photographs and artwork with excerpts from books and articles about Amish life. Visual memorabilia in general may also prove useful for memoirs and other creative nonfiction projects.

DEVELOPING AN IDEA INTO A STORY

A great deal is going on cognitively when a writer attempts to develop a full-fledged story out of an idea. For some experienced writers, much of that cognitive activity takes place semiconsciously. Consider driving a car: You don't actually consciously decide to move your foot from accelerator to brake (or, for manual transmissions, manipulating both feet among clutch, brake, and accelerator). The act of driving involves sublimating the many separate actions that constitute vehicle operation, as well as navigating through traffic, into a single act. The same holds true for writing. Until you have spent as many hours at your keyboard as you have behind the wheel, it will be necessary for you to be fully conscious of each stage of the composing process. For many writers the stages might be described as follows:

- Idea recognition stage
- Idea incubation stage
- Synopsis, plot outline stage
- Research stage
- Drafting stage
- Revision stage

Moreover, each of these separate stages consists of multiple smaller stages. The story construction stage, for example, consists of orchestrating specific incidents, each incident possessing its own dynamic mix of people and activity spread over time.

MAINTAINING A WRITER'S NOTEBOOK

Having read this far, you now have a better understanding of the idea-to-story process. Stories rarely appear full-blown in a writer's mind so that the writer simply needs to take mental dictation. If you can write like that, count your blessings and get to work; you don't need this book. Far more commonly, a writer gets an idea—or a fragment of an idea, jots it down, and spends the next several days or weeks or months or even years working it to fruition. It's a complex process, quite often a messy one. So it makes good sense to keep a notebook where all of these spontaneous thoughts and plans and research notes can be easily accessed.

Why are notebooks important? As the distinguished essayist Phillip Lopate writes in his foreword to *Writers and Their Notebooks*, edited by Diana M. Raab (University of South Carolina Press, 2010), the successful, genre-spanning authors in this anthology regard their notebooks (or journals) in many different ways . . .

> . . . as a laboratory, a mirror, a brainstorming tool, an icebreaker, a wailing wall, a junk drawer, a confessional, a postcard to oneself, singing in the shower, a playground for the mind, a jump-start cable, a memory aid, an archive, an anthology, a warehouse, a tourist's camera, a snooping device, a role-playing arena, an observation-sharpener, a survival kit.

Novelist, TV scriptwriter, and memoirist James Brown, in the lead essay, "Journaling—A Stepping Stone," regards his notebook as a tool that "can help the writer come up with ideas, kind of a warm-up to a bigger process. The next step," Brown goes on to explain, "is building on those ideas. . . . Story begins when you begin to dream and brainstorm about people and their problems."

What kind of notebook works best? I strongly recommend a loose-leaf one, kept in a binder at least 1½ inches deep, which will hold about four hundred pages. Why loose-leaf? Three reasons:

1. You can add or remove notes as you see fit.
2. You won't have to rip out pages as you would with notebooks with sewn or wire bindings.
3. You can easily rearrange your notebook's contents.

I should mention one limitation of the loose-leaf notebook: portability. If you're like me, ideas leap to mind at unexpected times, especially when traveling, so I find it prudent to carry a *pocket* notebook—one that I can quickly retrieve whenever an idea or clever thought strikes, when I simply want to make a verbal sketch of a street scene in a city I'm visiting, or when I want to take notes on museum exhibits or sit on a park bench and jot down story ideas about the people walking past. Over the years, I have filled dozens of such pocket notebooks, and I have fun mining them from time to time. Thoughts we found intriguing but didn't know how to develop when we first recorded them may suddenly seem easy to fashion into a story or essay. Of course, the reverse is also true; our interests and abilities are continually in flux.

In order to keep track of which notebook includes which notes, you can add cross-referencing glosses—e.g., "plot outline for this idea in large notebook"—or you can pull your notes from the pocket notebook and tape them into the large one. I personally do both; I also on occasion *expand* my original pocket-notebook jottings for the larger notebook.

To ensure that your notebook can function as a *workbook*—that is, as an efficient, well-organized resource for the different types of notes you will need for your short story, novel, or memoir in progress, I recommend injecting some color—literally—into the endeavor. Some writers, myself included, like to use pastel-colored filler paper as dividers within the notebook, a different color for each category you come up with. Why color? For one thing, colors enliven what could otherwise seem like drab busywork. Colors remind you that creative writing is a form of play—sophisticated play, to be sure, but play in the sense of being free-spirited and whimsical nonetheless.

There is, of course, a more practical aspect to color coding: The different colors will help you quickly reference the different types of notes you'll inevitably consult during the drafting process. Accessing needed information rapidly will eliminate hours of inefficient and frustrating rummaging through disorganized notes.

How best to organize your notebook? You may want to experiment, but I recommend using this scheme for starters: The color suggestions are, of course, subjective.

- Heuristic (Idea Generating) or Prewriting Activities (yellow pages)
- Character Profiles (beige pages)

- Outlines and Synopses (blue pages)
- Descriptions of Settings (green pages)
- Action Scenes (orange pages)
- Collages (blank white pages)
- Research Notes (lined white pages)

IDEA GENERATING OR BRAINSTORMING ON PAPER

One of the commonest causes of writer's block is what I call premature perfectionism—a kind of obsessive-compulsive disorder whereby every sentence has to be perfectly executed before it even hits the page, every word absolutely *le mot juste*, every paragraph chiseled out of Carrera marble. Such premature perfectionists are lucky to finish a paragraph during a single stint at the keyboard. Is it any wonder they are likely to find writing akin to self-flagellation? Not surprisingly, many such writers give up writing altogether. Here are a few tricks of the trade to get your creative imagination up and running.

GENERATING IDEAS BY FREE-ASSOCIATING

One relatively easy way to break through writer's block is to let your thoughts gush forth without restraint through free-associating (or brainstorming) on paper on a potential story idea, no matter how nebulous that idea may be. If your idea is the discovery of a mysterious hidden treasure in your backyard, then begin writing free-associatively about what comes to mind when you think of "buried treasure": gold coins hundreds of years old? Pirates? Jewels? But don't limit yourself to the usual associations; write down what comes to mind when you think about things that get buried or things that can qualify as "treasures." You might wind up with a string of associations that have little to do with buried treasure of the pirate variety—and that's what exercising your imagination is all about.

GENERATING IDEAS BY LISTING

Listing is a fun way of accumulating ideas for stories because it serves as a glimpse into human nature, into natural phenomena. List your favorite movies (later you can return to the list and explain why you like those movies); list five toys you enjoyed playing with as a child (later explain why you enjoyed each toy)—you can spend days and weeks preparing lists of all sorts, from favorite foods, books, or composers to most intriguing moments in history to things-I-must-do-before-I-die lists—and return to the lists any time to add the explanations.

GENERATING IDEAS BY MAPPING

Once you've generated useful lists of objects, incidents, and ideas, it is relatively easy to make connections among them through a brainstorming process known as mapping.

Story elements often occur to writers in cause-effect, temporal, or spatial relationships. Mapping is similar to free-associating, but with more emphasis on making connections to create an embryonic story progression.

GENERATING IDEAS BY CREATING
CHARACTER PROFILES

People are the lifeblood of any story. To put it another way, any story is a story about people. They may take a backseat to plot or idea, but even the most plot-centered or philosophical tale emanates from the needs of a central character. For that reason, the creation of vivid, realistic, unforgettable characters should be your prime directive when working up a story idea. Start by profiling your characters separately in your notebook. Include a wealth of details, more than you will most likely need, about your characters' physical appearances, behavioral characteristics (including eccentricities), ethnic backgrounds, family histories, childhood experiences, life-changing events, and so on. Remember that you are also practicing observation techniques here. The more closely you observe, the more you will see. Specific physical and sensory details are what help inject life into creative writing.

PLOT OUTLINES, SYNOPSES

Armed with an embryonic story scheme produced through free association, together with a sense of the characters who will move the story forward, you now should be able to work up a preliminary plot. Be prepared to go through several drafts of your synopsis before you're satisfied. The more details—the particular twists and turns you want the story to take to keep readers engrossed—the better.

Although some writers like to invent plot twists and turns as they go along, a much more efficient strategy—efficient in that it reduces the likelihood of false starts or dead ends—is to outline those twists and turns ahead of time. You can always revise the outline later, which almost always becomes necessary once the drafting process gets underway.

A useful preliminary to outlining is *mapping* (discussed in Chapter 5), a tentative means of establishing relationships among the story elements. After spontaneously listing possible story ingredients (also discussed in Chapter 5), a logical next step would be to use items in the list to fashion causal, temporal, or spatial connections. Of course, if you've already had some experience creating stories, you may find these activities somewhat elementary; but even experienced writers like to plan carefully—and that means taking small steps such as those featured in this book.

SETTINGS

Plot structure and story setting are inseparable. If you're going to write a story about the Mob during Prohibition, you will also need to set the action in one of the cities in which the Mob operated, such as Chicago. That would mean researching the Chicago of the 1930s to the point where you could describe it vividly and convincingly. Think of a story's setting as a character in its own right, possessing a distinctive appearance, its own personality, its own ever-changing moods. Remember, too, that you're writing notebook sketches, not drafting the story—so let yourself go. You might come up with descriptions of settings that won't be suitable to the story in progress but could be ideal for the next story you write.

RESEARCH NOTES

The very word *research* leaves some writers cold; it conjures up hours of tedious and time-consuming busywork inside a library. But research can be fascinating once you have some idea of the information you need. Thanks to the Internet, you can obtain basic background information about any topic in just a few minutes—but that's only the starting point. If you hope to immerse your readers in the reality of your story world, you must go beyond the preliminaries—beyond what can be extracted from Internet sites, even beyond library resources. That is, you need to conduct field research. Does your story include a scene in a hospital emergency room? You need to feel what it is like inside one so that you can convey those sensations to your readers. In this instance, research involves visiting an emergency room, talking to doctors and nurses about equipment and protocols, maybe reading memoirs by E.R. surgeons and nurses.

One last point I wish to make about maintaining a writer's notebook: The very act of recording your thoughts and observations, story plans, and outlines is self-rewarding. Notebook keeping helps train you to think like a writer, to pay close attention to what is going on in the world, to sharpen your powers of observation, and to feel comfortable with the physical act of translating thoughts and observations into words on paper.

DRAFTING

Writing a first draft can come at any time, even before the activities I refer to as pre-drafting (discussed in Chapters 4–6). Some writers will begin a draft—what rhetoricians like to call a *discovery draft*—and then feel the need to do some pre-drafting activities to get a better handle on their story idea. Also, it isn't necessary to draft a story from beginning to end. Some writers like to draft the ending first and to have everything else they write lead up to it. Other writers prefer to start somewhere in the middle and take turns working backwards and forwards. And some writers like to start with a scene—a confrontation between hero and villain, or a suspense-filled moment when your hero and an associate work desperately to locate and defuse a time bomb, say. It's quite likely, by the way, that you won't be using some or even most of the scenes you write for the particular story in progress. Thanks to your notebook, you can save the scenes you don't use now for a later project. Also thanks to your notebook, you can revise your scenes as often as you wish before inserting them into your story.

FOR YOUR WRITER'S NOTEBOOK

1. Take a walk, preferably in some unfamiliar place, pocket notebook in tow, and jot down sights, sounds, smells. Don't be concerned with capturing the unusual or being eloquent. You're simply after raw data. When you get home, expand some of your jottings into paragraphs on loose-leaf paper. Keep these pages in a separate section labeled "Miscellaneous Jottings."

2. What do you care most about? Being an effective parent? Rising to the top in your profession? Mastering a musical instrument (including your singing voice)? Whatever it is, write a letter to your spouse, closest friend, or other confidant, explaining why you care so much about this.

3. Write spontaneously on one or more of the following topics. Aim to fill at least two pages (about twenty minutes) on each topic.
   - A wedding reception
   - First day on the job
   - Signs that a house is haunted
   - Who am I?
   - Why do I want to be a writer?

- Raising a child
- A family reunion
- A mistake I wish I could undo

4. Compose a paragraph on one or more of the following prompts:
    - A strange person I know
    - An embarrassing moment
    - My three greatest pet peeves
    - My most memorable teachers
    - A dangerous situation I've been in

5. Take a mental inventory on all that you already know about . . .
    - Ancient Rome
    - Poker (or any other card or board game that you're familiar with)
    - Spiders
    - Greek myths
    - Psychoanalysis
    - Firearms
    - Women's or men's fashions (past or present)

6. After completing your mental inventory of what you know about one of the subjects in number 5 above, research the subject and list all of the new things you've learned.

   Prepare a one-page character sketch for each of the following individuals. Be sure to include both physical and behavioral characteristics, habits, hobbies, obsessions, strengths, and weaknesses.
    - One of your cousins
    - A grandparent
    - A girl or boy with whom you were infatuated in junior high school
    - A weird neighbor
    - An influential teacher

7. Write out five story ideas, one sentence for each idea. Next, take one of these one-sentence story ideas and expand it into a paragraph.

8. Get out scissors, paste, and some construction paper and create a collage of images, drawn from newspapers and magazines, which seem relevant to the short story, memoir, or novel you'd like to write.

CHAPTER 2

Where to Look for Ideas and How to Recognize Them

A writer's material is what he cares about. —JOHN GARDNER

"Ideas for stories are everywhere." You've heard that a thousand times—and it's true. Of course, you will find some places more promising than others for idea searching, depending on your interests. But more important, unless you deliberately seek out ideas and become able to recognize ideas with story potential, they will remain invisible, not unlike those figures camouflaged in children's fun-book drawings—squirrels intermingled with tree leaves, birds entwined in the whorls of clouds.

FINDING IDEAS IN BOOKS

One of the great pleasures of reading is that it extends not only our knowledge of the world, but our experience of it as well, especially our experience with people. It is not firsthand experience, of course, but *vicarious* experience, which, I hasten to add, should never be disparaged. ("You don't learn about life through books, Son.") We truly can learn about life through books, we can experience what it is like to be in someone else's shoes through books, and we can come to a deeper appreciation of human nature through the magic of reading.

No matter what subject areas interest you as a writer, immerse yourself in as many books on those subjects as you can. Reading both enhances existing interests and stimulates new interests. Your brain becomes a sponge for ideas when you read, so you'll want to keep your writer's notebook within reach. Let me share a case in point from my own recent reading of Jeffery Deaver's thriller set in 1936 Berlin, *Garden of Beasts* (2005), about an American assassin hired to take out a high-ranking Nazi official. This is the sort of novel that not only entertains you with a tension-filled, complex plot, but allows you to experience Berlin through all of your senses, *and* at the same time it gives you an education in the early history of World War II. I found myself jotting down several ideas, for example:

- Ethnic diversity among the Olympic athletes (e.g., the African-American runner Jesse Owens, a character in the novel) in ironic contrast to Hitler's Aryan racial policies
- Effect of the Gestapo and the SS on everyday society
- How the slenderest threads of forensic evidence can help solve a crime
- How Nazis achieved widespread adulation despite their brutality

It is also important to expand your repertoire of interests by reading about subjects to which you would not normally gravitate. As a writer, you want to be as knowledgeable in as many subjects as possible, for you never know when you may need to imbue your characters with expertise in matters that you yourself know little or nothing about. But before you begin circumnavigating the public library in a quest for omniscience, I recommend doing some in-depth character profiling so that you'll be able to limit your scope to what is necessary. If one of your characters is a private investigator, for example, take the time to read about the way actual PIs do their jobs—and ask questions

("What would happen if your detective continues to investigate a case the police have made off-limits to him?" "How will your detective secure the cooperation of the coroner?" and so on). And, of course, read novels in which private investigators do their thing—works by Lawrence Block, Jane Langton, Robert Parker, Ruth Rendell, and the like. Don't just read their novels for story alone; study them carefully to see how each plot builds around a core idea, how one event sets the stage for the next, and how the relationships between characters develop from chapter to chapter.

FINDING IDEAS IN REFERENCE WORKS

We not only read books but consult them for specific kinds of information and inspiration. Encyclopedias, almanacs, handbooks, dictionaries—all kinds of dictionaries—user manuals, compendiums of anecdotes, letters, and so forth are endless resources for raw ideas. Let's start with dictionaries: It is quite possible to come up with a story idea simply from looking up the definition of an unfamiliar word in your shopworn desk dictionary, or a bizarre word such as those found in *Mrs. Byrne's Dictionary of Unusual, Obscure and Preposterous Words* (compiled by Josefa Heifetz Byrne, daughter of the renowned violinist Jascha Heifetz). Take for instance the word *godling*—which Mrs. Byrne's Dictionary defines as "a puny or small-time god." Did a story idea suddenly leap to mind? It made me imagine a children's story in which a group of godlings are sulking about, unhappy that no one pays them the kind of attention they feel they deserve . . . until one of them thinks of a way to upstage Aphrodite or Poseidon, or any of the other Olympian big shots.

By the way, mythological dictionaries, such as J.E. Zimmerman's *Dictionary of Classical Mythology,* or the more elaborate and lavishly illustrated *Myths: Tales of the Greek and Roman Gods* by Lucia Impelluso, are terrific idea generators. Like Bible stories, the ancient myths and legends offer rich thematic material to contemporary fiction.

Here is an especially fascinating reference resource: a compendium of anonymous confessional letters. In his book *Post Secret: Extraordinary Confessions from Ordinary Lives* (2005), Frank Warren reproduces hundreds of the startling secrets complete strangers sent him, often (per his direction) artistically presented. Here are three such secrets:

- I waste office supplies because I hate my boss
- I hate getting older . . . you know more than you ever wanted to know
- I trashed my parents' house to look like I had a party while they were out of town, so my mom would think I had friends

With a bit of imagination, you could use any of these secrets as the core idea for a heart-rending short story.

A similar reference work, *Dear Old Love* (2009), compiled by Andy Selsberg, collects hundreds of anonymous messages addressed to former loves. Many of them beautifully capture in a nutshell the hurt, the humiliation, the wistful pleasures of a romantic relationship that has ended. Here is a sampling:

- I was afraid if you got close, you'd see the Scotch tape holding me together
- You were the only worthwhile thing I studied in college
- I liked your roommate better

FINDING IDEAS IN NEWSPAPERS AND MAGAZINES

If you're like me, there's no such thing as too much reading material. Not only is my house swimming in books, it's swimming in periodicals of all kinds—newspapers, literary journals, scientific and cultural affairs magazines. Why subscribe to so many print periodicals in this digital age, you ask? Well, I enjoy *print*: It has material presence, it won't vanish if the computer crashes, and besides, I enjoy clipping and filing the pieces that interest me and that could someday spark an idea for a story or essay, poem, or play. Of course, you can use the Internet for this simply by printing out documents or storing them on your computer.

Sometimes an idea will strike me when I first read an article, in which case I'll grab my notebook and capture the idea in a brief paragraph before it fades away. Most of the time, though, an article that catches my attention will not yield a story idea right away; but a week or a year later it very well could. For that reason it makes sense to create an efficient filing system.

Here is what I do: I purchase stackable, sturdy plastic filing cabinets (the ones with slide-out drawers), and arrange the clippings in manila envelopes by subject. A few of my file-folder headings include the following:

- Scientific discoveries; inventions
- Health and medicine
- Sports and recreation
- War, espionage
- Heroic, altruistic deeds
- Crises, disasters
- Crimes
- Religious experiences, controversies

Every so often, especially when I'm between projects, I'll flick through some of these files, ready to capture any sparks that fly. Here's an article, in my "Far Out Ideas" folder, about smart dresses—no, not smart as in "smartly dressed" but smart as in smartphone. Anne Eisenberg in her article "Which Way to the Ball? I'll Ask My Gown" (*The New York Times*, Feb. 26, 2012) describes garments that incorporate electronics—for example, dresses with LEDs embedded in the fabric that "shine more intensely as the wearer moves." Spark! I grabbed my notebook to capture a sudden idea: *What if clothes became "smart" enough to acquire wills of their own and began controlling the people who wore them in ways the wearers never anticipated?*

Dipping into my "Health and Medicine" folder, I come across an article about seriously injured veterans who engage in extreme sports—and by the way, you'll notice a lot of cross-referencing possibilities: This article could just as well have been filed under "Sports and Recreation." Anyway, the writer, A.G. Sulzberger, describes how one of these vets, former Marine Darol Kubacz, a paraplegic, turned to custom-wheelchair paragliding (via a program paid for with grants from the Paralyzed Veterans of America and the Christopher and Dana Reeve Foundation). Can you conjure up a story idea from this? This is what I jotted down: "Story about a paralyzed veteran who engages in paragliding—not just to compensate for his paralysis, but in a desperate effort to overcome the horrors he experienced on the battlefield."

One more point about getting ideas from periodicals: It doesn't take much to trigger an idea for a story once you've deployed your idea radar. Sometimes a title alone will do the job—like "The Asylum Seeker," by Suketu Mehta (*The New Yorker*, August 1, 2011), about the challenge of new immigrants to find a better life in the United States, and how emphasizing their traumatic experiences in their native lands can help. Reading the article will bring up all kinds of ideas, of course, but the title itself was enough for me to jot down: "Story set in the 1940s about a free-thinking immigrant from a repressive regime that arouses suspicions and ironically gets confined in a state mental hospital." (A play on the word *asylum*, you see.)

EMBARKING ON AN IDEA SAFARI

Invaluable as reading is, it cannot be the sum and substance of a writer's experience. Even famous literary recluses like J.D. Salinger experienced life directly and abundantly before they became recluses. If you are a homebody (not the same as a recluse), you can find countless ideas from your immediate surroundings to write about: preparing unusual recipes, training pets, growing exotic flowers, or tackling how-to projects like replacing bathroom faucets or adding more shelf space in your garage or closets. If fiction is your calling, you might gravitate toward writing a series of haunted house stories, or psycho-dramas about dysfunctional family life.

Exploring the outdoors or interior spaces other than your own home, naturally, will expand the possibilities for finding ideas. That is why so many writers love to travel. There's something truly adventur-ous about entering an unfamiliar country, a strange city, a way of life very different from your own, that heightens the senses and expands one's understanding of human culture—which is just what you want to have happen. Make sure you keep a pocket notebook handy when-ever you embark on what I like to call idea safaris so you can capture as many sights, sounds, and smells as you experience them; you never know what can lead to an idea for a story. For example, say that you vis-it, as I once did, the ruins of ancient Pompeii—the town that had been buried for centuries under volcanic ash and rock after Mount Vesuvi-us erupted in A.D. 79. At first I was overwhelmed by all that I saw; but after a while I took notes on particulars with the greatest potential for story ideas (the tour guide helped me focus). Here are a few excerpts:

- Grooves in the stone streets carved by decades of wagon traf-fic—still visible.
- Ruins of a bakery, bread oven still intact
- Rows of houses, mostly still intact except for the roofs
- One large home with spacious atrium and wall frescoes
- A brothel, with wall frescoes depicting, in embarrassing detail, the god Priapus in a state of, well, readiness; teenagers in the tour group giggling; parents not amused
- The mold of a mother protecting her infant child as the volca-nic ash asphyxiated them
- Specter of the dormant Mount Vesuvius looming in the distance

Each one of these impressions could, through free association (see Chapter 3), generate story possibilities.

A quick aside about cameras: Though it's fun to create a photographic record of your adventures, and visual images help generate ideas, writing is better because the more you translate experiences into language, the more adept a writer you will become. And besides, the sensory immediacy you will most likely capture in your jottings could prove valuable when it is time to create a vicarious experience for your readers.

MASTERING THE FINE ART OF IDEA RECOGNITION

Even if ideas strike you head-on, they will not take hold in your mind unless you are determined to approach them as ideas you care about. By that, I mean you must be motivated to explore them in depth, through writing. How often, after being reminded of some harsh experience (the difficulties of raising children; surviving in a dysfunctional workplace; enduring a mercurial romance), have you proclaimed, "Oh, I could write a book about that!" And you most likely could, except that you don't take yourself seriously when you say it. Why is that? Most likely it's either lack of confidence (you assume that you don't have the talent or that only literary geniuses can write books); or that it would take you *forever* to fill four hundred pages, and you couldn't possibly invest so much time; or that you do not know how to begin writing a novel or memoir. Well, you do not need to be a genius or possess any special talent or have a year of free time; you can complete the task in much less time than you think, provided you work on it virtually every day; and as for not knowing how to begin, reading this book will show you how.

IDEA FISHING

The first step in learning to recognize ideas is to fish for them. I use the metaphor quite deliberately. Imagine that you're out fishing on a lake. Until you bait your hook and cast your line, the possibility of encountering any fish is nil; no way are they going to jump into your boat. How you bait your hook and how and where (and often when) you cast your line, will determine whether you'll catch a fish, or even what kind.

Now then, you've heard the saying that there are all kinds of fish in the sea. Some fish are relatively ordinary or not good to eat or too tiny. The same is true of ideas: many of the ideas you "catch" will not be worth writing about because they're not very interesting or they are insignificant. So you keep casting your line and before long you'll reel in something promising. Don't be too hasty in your judgment, though. Great ideas may seem quite modest at first. Say you're rereading L. Frank Baum's *The Wonderful Wizard of Oz* and you find yourself wishing you knew more about the Wicked Witch of the West. After a moment, the thought fades away; but if you were Gregory Maguire, you would have run with that idea, creating the best-selling novel, *Wicked: The Life and Times of the Wicked Witch of the West*, which resulted in a Tony Award winning Broadway musical. Moral of that story: When fishing for ideas, don't overlook the possibility of using classic works of literature, folklore, fairy tales, and myths as springboards for "spin-offs." Other examples of deriving new ideas from old ones include Tom Stoppard's *Rosencrantz and Guildenstern Are Dead* (which reconceptualizes *Hamlet* from the point of view of that play's two most insignificant characters); and *My Fair Lady* (which reconceptualizes George Bernard Shaw's *Pygmalion*, which in turn reconceptualizes the Greek myth).

Another kind of "idea fish" is one that arises from a distinctive experience, one from which you learn a valuable lesson—but also one from which many persons could learn a valuable lesson too. In fact, whenever you're idea fishing, ask yourself: Would this idea be of interest to a wide audience? At the risk of overstating the obvious, always remember that the whole point of writing for publication is to be read.

But how do you learn to recognize ideas that do not come to you in a flash? Aside from the obvious—make an *effort* to look for them (seek and ye shall find!)—I recommend keeping four things in mind:

1. Pay close attention to what you would otherwise gloss over
2. Ask questions about the things you observe

3. Pay special attention to the things that you care most about or those that most arouse your curiosity
4. Capture the resulting ideas, however tentative, in your notebook

Let's look at each of these idea-recognition strategies in detail.

PAYING CLOSE ATTENTION

Actively seeking out ideas means more than just telling yourself, "Okay, today I'm going to go out and find an idea for a novel," as if novel ideas are out there for the plucking, hidden or camouflaged like mushrooms or chameleons. As a writer in training, make an effort to heighten curiosity and a sense of wonder about your surroundings, keeping in mind that *everything* is more than what it seems at first glance. How do you heighten your curiosity about things? By paying close attention—to anything and everything. Do not limit your observations at first; sharpening focus will become necessary later on. Even if you intend to write strictly commercial genre fiction—mysteries, thrillers, romances, fantasies, westerns—you must heighten your ability to notice details and nuances, so that when you begin drafting your stories, you'll remember to give your settings, characters, and events the ring of authenticity that only plentiful, specific details can give.

Seeking ideas actively rather than passively reminds me of the distinction between gathering food (or growing it; i.e., agriculture) and hunting for it. If you're at the mercy of only what is available, you'll starve when that food source disappears—say, because of extinction or drought. You may recall the opening moments of Stanley Kubrick and Arthur C. Clarke's epic science fiction film, *2001: A Space Odyssey*: The proto-humans are desperately plucking leaves and berries from an arid terrain that had once been lush, oblivious to the wild game surrounding them. But then overnight the aliens plant their inscrutable monolith, which imbues the most promising of the man-apes with the kind of insight that will transform humanity: Crouched beside a heap of bones he is suddenly able to envision how a bone can function as a tool and a weapon, and how the warthogs surrounding him are potential food. Hunger and survival are the true forces behind this idea recognition; the monolith is only a prod, a catalyst, sort of like a good teacher who coaches from the sidelines rather than instructs, thereby giving her students just enough guidance to enable them to draw from *their* inner resources, not the teacher's. External necessity (striving to win the game, to continue the sports metaphor) is crucial, but it is not sufficient; athletes must also learn to most effectively exploit their unique resources—their own unique combination of skill, endurance, and competitive zeal. To put it more bluntly: You can read a zillion books on how to become a successful writer; but unless you care deeply about writing for its own sake, none of that instruction will take hold.

We assume that seeing is the most natural activity there is—all you need to do is keep your eyes open. But that is only half true. Yes, if you focus on a particular scene, you technically see everything that's there, much the way a camera lens captures everything within its focal range. But whereas a camera eye is pure reception (aside from the fact that the photographer controls such variables as angle, light and shadow, shutter speed, film speed, and so forth), the human eye (being connected to the human brain) almost inevitably imbues a given scene with associations that make the object more meaningful. For example, the camera eye sees a desert road trailing off into the distance; but the (attentive) human eye may see not just the road and the surrounding desert, but particulars: certain types of rocks, for example, that in turn suggest the presence of minerals or gemstones.

Moreover, there is such a thing as *emotional* attentiveness. A road winding through the Rocky Mountains will convey to some a vision of rugged wilderness, of nature's majesty and permanence, of America the Beautiful. Even a flat, featureless Midwestern prairie can be evocative in the hands of a skilled storyteller. Whereas a nonwriter might only see a flat, empty, and very boring landscape, a skilled writer-observer like L. Frank Baum would see much more. Here is how Baum, through Dorothy's eyes, perceives the Kansas prairie:

> When Dorothy stood in the doorway and looked around, she could see nothing but the great gray prairie on every side. Not a tree nor a house broke the broad sweep of flat country that reached the edge of the sky in all directions. The sun had baked the plowed land into a gray mass, with little cracks running through it. Even the grass was not green, for the sun had burned the tops of the long blades until they were the same gray color to be seen elsewhere.

By evoking the scene with concrete details (the gray mass of the sun-baked plowed land; the little cracks in the ground; the gray, sun-scorched blades of grass), Baum reminds us how observing even ordinary things can be a creative act, not just a physiological one.

As a writer, though, you want more than just emotional impressions from the things you observe; you want to see story possibilities in them—or, if you already have a story in mind, you want to see how a particular setting can contribute to the story. The dreary Kansas prairie surrounding Dorothy's home serves as a dramatic contrast to the colorful and magical land of Oz she will soon be whisked to by a cyclone.

But, you may be wondering, what steps can one take to become adept at recognizing story potential in one's surroundings? First, you must condition yourself into letting a given object *remind* you of things—of experiences, other objects. After all, everything can be connected to everything else. A city bus may remind you of the time when you could not afford a car and had to rely on mass transportation to get around; or it may remind you of the need for improved mass transit in your community; or it may remind you of early efforts to desegregate public schools by busing students from one school to another. "Seeing," in this context, is a kind of visual free-associating, what I like to think of as "whole brain" observation. The more you see this way, the easier it becomes.

ASKING QUESTIONS ABOUT
WHAT YOU OBSERVE

Questioning helps bring ideas into focus because it leads to better understanding and insight into the nature of things. To question is to embark on a *quest* for new knowledge (and yes, the words are etymologically related—from the Latin *quaerere*, to ask or seek; the words *inquiry* and *query* also stem from this Latin term). Consider the following everyday example of how a questioning mind can help bring out story possibilities in ideas.

Picture an elderly gentleman seated on a park bench looking forlorn and displaced. This may not seem like a promising basis for a story if you simply regard the man unquestioningly; but if you shift your imagination into high gear and ask a question about the gentleman, potential ideas for stories will materialize. For example, you might ask: Who is this old man, and why is he sitting by himself, looking so forlorn? The question (actually three questions embedded into one) becomes a prod for all sorts of ideas if you allow yourself to be imaginative:

- The elderly gentleman is actually a wizard who fell out of favor with his people and has been exiled to live out his days among ordinary folk; he wants to return to his world, to once again win the hearts of his people
- He is a World War II or Korean War veteran who never received the recognition he felt he deserved for a heroic deed; but soon, a long-lost fellow vet from his platoon, whose life the old man saved, will walk by and recognize him
- The old man has spent most of his life hiding a terrible secret, but he is now ready to divulge it to the right person

Questioning is also important in story development, which we'll say more about when we get to plotting; but for now, take another look at these scenarios: Each of them generates a host of more specific questions that can lead you toward shaping a storyline. Let's further probe the third scenario—the gentleman has been hiding a terrible secret. That answer begets a long string of questions, all of which have the potential to build into a story:

- What is the secret?
- Why did he keep the secret for so long without telling anyone?
- Who is going to be the right person to tell it to?
- What will that person do with the secret once he or she hears it?

Questioning, then, plays a formative role in transforming a raw idea into a story premise. It is not just an isolated step but also a fundamental aspect of critical thinking that will bear fruit throughout the composing process, including revising and copyediting the final draft.

SCRUTINIZING THE THINGS YOU CARE MOST ABOUT

Each of us cares about a lot of things, and with varying degrees of caring—from caring about keeping our desks tidy to devoting our lives to a great humanitarian cause. Also, what we didn't care about yesterday we may care a great deal about tomorrow. As writers-in-training the more we find things to care about, the more readily we will recognize potential ideas for stories.

Back up a moment and reflect on what it is that gets you to care about something:

- It stirs your emotions
- It draws you in, motivates you to become involved
- It arouses your curiosity, puts you in a questioning mode
- It kindles your imagination
- It stirs up memories, experiences

Writers need to feel strongly about, and be motivated to learn all they can about, the professional milieu their characters inhabit. Without that intense degree of caring, you may be tempted to oversimplify, to overlook inconspicuous but necessary details and nuances that would add dimensionality and verisimilitude to the world you're aiming to create on paper. A mystery writer, for instance, must be both fascinated and knowledgeable about crime investigation (public and/or private) and the criminal mind; a romance writer must find endless fascination with the emotional tsunamis of conflicted love and the motives for betrayal; the fantasy writer should be utterly enchanted with magic and magical lands. Only with that kind of motivation will the invisible ideas surrounding you become visible.

CAPTURING IDEAS IN YOUR NOTEBOOK

Writing down your thoughts, however amorphous, is important because the very effort to capture ideas in words helps to develop them.

One of the most fascinating things about becoming an active idea hunter is that the very act of hunting for ideas will sharpen both your observational skills and your imaginative skills. Work hard to cultivate the habit of writing down the ideas you've hunted down, even before you begin assessing their story potential.

FOR YOUR WRITER'S NOTEBOOK

1. Here's an opportunity to practice idea recognition while simultaneously doing housework: Find a cluttered closet, junk drawer, or corner of your attic, garage, or basement, and organize it. As you do so, see how many potential story ideas you can recognize in the items you come across. Here are two examples from a closet purging to get you going:
   - Old musical audiotapes from a long-forgotten jazz quartet. Possible idea: What if a jazz enthusiast, recognizing

the exceptional talent of this group, sets out to find the individual musicians and reunite them?

- A cache of holiday greetings from twenty years ago, some from friends and relatives you haven't heard from since or have since fallen out of favor. Possible idea: What would happen if your main character attempted to reestablish a close friendship (implicit in one of the old greeting cards) that had gone sour for whatever reason?

2. Write out two or more potential ideas for stories set in the modern world based on the following account by Thomas Bullfinch of the myth of Phaeton:

> Phaeton was the son of Apollo and the nymph Clymene. One day a schoolfellow laughed at the idea of his being the son of the god, and Phaeton went in rage and shame and reported it to his mother. "If," said he, "I am indeed of heavenly birth, give me, mother, some proof of it. . . ." Clymene stretched forth her hands towards the skies . . . "Go and demand of him [the sun god Apollo] whether he will own you as a son."

3. Read a human interest feature in your daily newspaper (print or online) and describe how you would turn that feature into a short story. For example, in a *New York Times* feature for July 27, 2011, Ethan Bronner describes how a group of Israeli women risked arrest by smuggling a group of Palestinian women out of the land-locked southern section of the West Bank and bringing them to an Israeli beach for a day of fun and frolic. "Skittish at first, then wide-eyed with delight, the women and girls entered the sea, smiling, splashing and then joining hands, getting knocked over by the waves, throwing back their heads and ultimately laughing with

joy. Most had never seen the sea before." What basic story idea could you extract from this delightful incident? Could you juxtapose it against the background of complex Israeli-Palestinian politics?

4. The next time you take a trip—whether abroad or to a nearby hiking trail—bring your pocket notebook and fill it with detailed observations. Be sure to include descriptions of sounds, smells, and tactile sensations as well as sights. When you get home, generate two or three story ideas from at least one of those observations.

5. Take an inventory of several things you care deeply about; categorize your inventory as follows: arts (visual, literary, performance); social issues; recreational activities; family life; spiritual concerns. Select one item from each category to shape into a story idea. Examples:

   • Jazz. Idea: Intertwined lives of Dixieland jazz musicians who come together at Preservation Hall in New Orleans.
   • Wilderness excursion. Idea: After three buddies go hiking in rugged terrain and get lost, their fun-filled adventure becomes a desperate struggle for survival.

6. Look up five of the weirdest words you've ever seen (such as those that appear in *Mrs. Byrne's Dictionary*). Work up a story idea based on one of the words or try weaving a story involving all five words.

7. Suggest a story idea for each of the following end-of-the-affair messages (taken from Andy Selsberg's *Dear Old Love*):

   • What I wouldn't give to feel awkward around you again.
   • I deserve better but I don't want better.

8. A dictionary of quotations, such as *The Oxford Dictionary of Quotations* or Bergen Evans's *Dictionary of Quotations*, is a veri-

table gold mine of ideas. Suggest a story idea based on one or more of the following quotations, taken from *The Oxford Dictionary of Quotations*:

- "You can tell a lot about a fellow's character by his way of eating jelly beans." —Ronald Reagan
- "Television is actually closer to reality than anything in books. The madness of TV is the madness of human life." —Camille Paglia

9. Grab a pocket notebook and stroll through your house, room by room. Jot down two ideas, one for fiction, the other for nonfiction, relating to the *history* of each object you encounter. Here are a few examples:

OBJECT	NONFICTION IDEA	FICTION IDEA
Lamp	Origin of electric table lamps	Family history from POV of heirloom lamp
Fireplace	How people kept warm before gas heat	Would-be burglar gets stuck in fireplace
Closet	Closet memorabilia from childhood	Love letters reveal a relative's secret past

10. Locate in a recent newspaper or magazine three articles that grab your attention. For each article, jot down at least two story ideas. They don't have to be directly connected to the article, but they should include a protagonist faced with a daunting conflict situation.

CHAPTER 3

Getting Ideas Out of the Blue

Discovery favors the well-prepared mind. —JEROME BRUNER

Now that you have a better sense of where to look for ideas and are better able to recognize story ideas anywhere you look, getting ideas should become second nature. Your powers of observation will have improved in the process, along with your ability to ask the kinds of questions about a nascent idea that will help turn it into a story.

Being able to recognize the ideas in your surroundings or in books lays the groundwork for conjuring up ideas out of the blue—from thought alone—and that is the focus of this chapter.

THINKING AND WRITING

Thinking is often dichotomized as either "critical" or "creative"; but it makes more sense to envision thinking as a spectrum, whereby any kind of thinking along the spectrum exhibits the characteristics of both critical and creative in varying degrees. No matter what kind of writing you're engaged in, from scientific analysis to fantasy, you need to think both creatively and critically.

It is difficult to overemphasize the importance of thinking in relation to writing. When he was interviewed at the 2011 National Book Festival in Washington, D.C., by C-SPAN's Book TV, the distinguished historian and biographer David McCullough pointed out that he is always asked how he balances research with writing but is never asked how much time he spends *thinking*—thinking about how discovery of new facts will affect his subject, or how to assimilate information into an engaging narrative, or how to go about re-creating a historical moment dramatically without sacrificing accuracy. Thinking is the force that transforms notions into narratives. One cannot be an effective writer, nor can one conjure up good ideas, without being able to think well—both critically and creatively.

Is it possible to improve one's thinking skills? Not only is it possible, it is also easy to do. I see four steps in the process:

FIRST STEP: Make a conscious effort to work on your thinking every day. That sounds kind of funny, but the mind, like the body, is strengthened by frequent exercise. There are times when I wish we had 24-hour cognitive fitness centers, where folks could get their brains in shape as zealously as they get their bodies in shape. Well, that may take a while; in the meantime, you can practice three exercises that will lead to excellent brain-muscle tone and definition—exactly what a budding writer needs to wrestle ideas into submission:

1. Regard every assumption you make as conditional, i.e., subject to later scrutiny.
2. Remember that every argument has at least one (and often several) counterarguments worth considering.
3. Challenge yourself to analyze complex issues on your own without relying on what other people have concluded, no matter how admirable or influential they are.

SECOND STEP: Identify any counterproductive thinking habits and get rid of them. Here are a few of the more commonplace kinds of counterproductive thinking:

- Insufficient time allotted for reflecting on incidents or concepts thoroughly
- Overlooking or ignoring nuances, subtleties
- Overlooking or ignoring historical contexts
- Failure to consider possible consequences of a person's (or fictional character's) actions or inactions
- Failure to experiment with alternatives
- Mistaking caricatures, stereotypes, or oversimplifications for indisputable truth

Dramatic improvement in your thinking skills will occur just by vanquishing the above six shortcomings. How do I do that, you may wonder? After all, old thinking habits are tough to get rid of. I recommend the following: First, identify and write down your bad thinking habits. Second, for the next couple of weeks or so, maintain a log of every cognitive "transgression." And finally, explain to yourself how to transform the flawed thinking into more effective thinking.

THIRD STEP: Pose questions before settling on assumptions. When I was an undergraduate during the sixties, a popular slogan button implored everyone to

QUESTION AUTHORITY

—the authority, for example, that lay behind unjust laws like the Volstead Act, which launched Prohibition; like the House Un-American Activities Committee hearings, which ordered Americans to testify against fellow Americans suspected of being subversives; like school segregation; like "Don't ask, don't tell," repealed in 2011. Every time an "authoritative" assumption enters your head, regardless of whether it is based on hearsay or on a law, *question* it. For our purposes here, think of the seemingly indisputable self-imposed assertions about authorship that you have adopted as gospel truth—e.g., "As long as I hold a full-time job, I don't have enough time to write." Now turn it into a question ("Is it possible for me to find time to write even though I work full time?") The act of questioning instantly puts you into a probing—a *questing*—state of mind.

A quick way to generate ideas (at least embryonic ones) out of the blue is to ask "what if" of any thought that enters your mind, no matter how mundane or trivial. You'll be amazed by the possible "story stuff" that comes into focus via this powerful question. Let's see how it works:

- Take the following utterly mundane thought: *The lawn needs to be mowed.*
- Now apply the "what if" question: What if I hired a neighbor's teenage kid to mow the lawn for me without his or her parents' consent? Possible story idea: The boy's (or girl's) parents, who have always held a grudge against the narrator (because of his political views? because he never displayed the Stars and Stripes on Memorial Day? because he didn't mow his lawn often enough? because his skin was a different color?) sues the narrator for child endangerment, triggering a feud. Possible emerging theme: Underneath the superficial courtesies and smiles, suspicion, intolerance for nonconformity, perhaps bigotry, lurk and flare into vindictiveness, even violence, at any pretext.

"What if" questions are the hallmark of science fiction and fantasy writers, of course. Even the most seemingly ordinary objects and events can suddenly become the basis for imaginative story scenarios when you pose this magical question. Mundane thought: Man buys an old-fashioned camera at a flea market. Imagination applied to mundane thought: What if that camera could take pictures of events that hadn't occurred yet? (You probably know how that one plays out: It is one of the original *Twilight Zone* episodes.)

FOURTH STEP: Look for ways to generate surprise and unexpectedness in your ideas. This will take you right to the heart of creative thinking. In his book, *Synectics* (1961), a guide to developing one's creativity in any professional activity, William J. J. Gordon argues that the process of creative problem solving involves "making the strange familiar" and "making the familiar strange." To accomplish the former, it is important to realize that, as Gordon explains, "the mind attempts to engorge . . . strangeness by forcing it into an acceptable pattern. . ." But the mind also craves the unexpected. Making the familiar strange, Gordon writes, "is the conscious attempt to achieve a new look at the same old world, people, ideas, feelings, and things." The education psychologist Jerome Bruner, in *On Knowing: Essays for the Left Hand* (1979), describes the response to strangeness as "effective surprise." By surprise Bruner means "The unexpected that strikes one with wonder or astonishment." Bruner goes on to explain that this kind of surprise is the result "of combinatorial activity—a placing of things in new perspectives"—and gives as an example, the sculptor Henry Moore's use of holes, which, he discovered, added a three-dimensionality to his solid forms.

It is possible to conjure up story ideas out of the blue like those mentioned above entirely in your head, but I recommend writing everything down in your notebook instead. Writing begets writing more efficiently than thinking begets thinking. Besides, if you're structuring a complex plot, ideas for the twists and turns typical of thrillers and mysteries will come to you more readily when you're writing them out. You may recall E.M. Forster's comment about the connection between thinking and writing: "How do I know what I think till I see what I say?" Even if you're working on a short story, you will need to be continually inventive. Your story may have evolved from a single idea, but that idea rapidly proliferates into subsidiary ideas as the characters and the circumstances become more complex than you have anticipated. The psychological forces underlying human motivation are sometimes too complex to anticipate; but once you are deeply into rendering your characters' actions and reactions, some of these subtle forces begin to surface—this is the phenomenon of characters "taking on a life of their own."

Every time you think about any aspect of your work in progress—character, plot, setting, theme, and so on, immediately begin jotting down "what if" questions pertaining to each aspect. For example, if you're writing a story about a homeowner who, while planting flowers in her backyard, digs up a leather pouch filled with documents, here is one way to generate ideas through what-if brainstorming in your notebook:

- Brainstorm about the different kinds of documents that might be in that leather pouch; later, select the most intriguing idea you came up with.
- Sketch a skeletal plot: What does the woman do with the document? Who else eventually learns about it?
- What if one of these persons wants the document for himself?

People sometimes say that life is a crapshoot: Everything that happens could have happened differently if just one tiny variable had been present. Imagine that you're writing a story about a young female ice-skater who learns she has qualified for the next Winter Olympic Games. *What if* your young woman narrator protagonist slips on an icy sidewalk and strains the tendons of her ankle? Will she still be able to train for the Olympics? If so, how? What if she meets a physical therapist who discourages her from competing? Complication (these are always important): They fall in love.

If you want to conjure up enough ideas to keep you writing for the next ten years, start thinking about the numerous junctures in your own life in which minor shifts in happenstance might have led to very different outcomes.

TALKING OUT AN IDEA

Conversation is a powerful heuristic (an aid to generating content)—no surprise, since talking is the way we use language most of the time, every day of our lives. Think about your oral language fluency for a moment. A typescript of a week's worth of conversation would fill a book, maybe two if your job requires you to give presentations or participate in meetings. Perhaps you've wished you could be as fluent with language on paper as you are with speech. It's all a matter of what you're accustomed to. Prolific writers are accustomed to writing as often as they speak—maybe more often. Isaac Asimov (1920–1992) published nearly five hundred books (science fiction novels, science essays, reference works, edited anthologies, and others)—more books than most people read during their adult lives. That's because Asimov loved to think and could think best through his fingertips, as he put it. Of course, not many of us can be as prolific as Asimov, nor would we want to be; but we can all learn to become more fluent with written language. Talking out our thoughts is a good way to make the transition.

Some writers argue that talking out a story idea could kill it; you would in effect be stealing your own thunder and lose the motivation to write it out. I, however, argue that in most cases the opposite is true. Assuming your idea has not fully taken shape, talking out an idea will help you to conceptualize it better, thanks to our lifelong experience with translating thoughts into speech. Also, the person or persons with whom you're conversing will likely prompt you with questions and suggestions. Here is a hypothetical scenario in which a writer talks out an idea with a friend:

> **WRITER:** I came up with this weird idea about a scientist who accidentally transfers his consciousness into the brain of a dog, but I'm not sure how to develop it.
> **FRIEND:** What kind of experiment was the scientist conducting?
> **WRITER:** Well, he was trying to determine the degree to which animals like dogs and other mammals exhibit reasoning ability. He was especially curious about dogs because they can learn to do some pretty awesome tasks.

FRIEND: Yeah, like how to save children from burning homes. But how does the scientist manage to get inside a dog's consciousness?

WRITER: I'm not worried about inventing some science-fictional gimmick to solve that problem. What I'm wondering about is (a) How will he be able to tell his wife and anyone else that his consciousness is now the dog's and—

FRIEND: Hey, what happens to the dog's consciousness?

WRITER: Maybe it goes into limbo.

FRIEND: Or maybe it becomes fused with the scientist's. Remember that horror flick *The Fly*?

WRITER: Wow, I like that idea!

As you can see, a focused conversation like that can prove to be fruitful very quickly.

HOW IDEAS PROLIFERATE

As I pointed out earlier, ideas beget ideas. Once you start thinking in earnest about a story idea, don't be surprised to discover that your brain starts swimming with a thousand related "spin-off" or subordinate ideas. Just as you learn more about people the more you interact with them, you will learn more about your characters the more you have them interact with other characters. In great works of literature, we find characters like Hester Prynne, Emma Bovary, Huck Finn, Jay Gatsby, Sherlock Holmes, and Scarlett O'Hara three-dimensional. They are as realistic as actual people because of the way their natures grow more complex when they interact with other characters. Your own characters will almost inevitably grow in complexity in your efforts to bring them across realistically. Every time you engage your character in some incident (or interaction with another character), new ideas come into play. Huck grows in complexity when we see him scheming to escape from his drunken Pap or when he meets up with river rogues and con artists during his raft trip down the Mississippi with his slave friend Jim. Every incident is an idea, and the cumulative effect of these incidents gives the story its thematic richness, its mythic quality.

Of course, many of your spin-off ideas will occur while you are drafting the story, not while you are sketching them out in your notebook. On the other hand, sketching them out before you have a plot structure going will serve as kindling for building a more imaginative, complex story than you might otherwise have imagined.

LETTING YOUR IMAGINATION RUN WILD

Speaking of imagination, most people, even aspiring writers, keep a tight leash on it. It's quite understandable: For many people, alas, an ungoverned imagination suggests lack of discipline, propriety, maturity. Modern society is basically pragmatic, no-nonsense. Flights of fancy are frowned upon, despite efforts in the corporate workplace to "think outside the box." What if you wanted to do away with the box altogether? You might get yourself fired.

But it's important to unhook the leash on your imagination, even to let it run wild just to see what it can come up with when the restraints are gone. Of course, an unrestrained imagination carries with it a certain degree of defiance, and disaffection, with the status quo. You may risk being regarded as a troublemaker, a loon. People may laugh at you the way they must have made fun of Wilbur and Orville Wright: "If we were meant to fly, we'd be born with wings!"

Okay, so the first thing to keep in mind when waxing imaginative is to grow a thick skin and don't be intimidated by the scoffers and scolders. Fill your brainstorming pages with crazy stuff. See what emerges that could contribute to a refreshingly original story. Reread a Harry Potter novel or two just to be reminded of J.K. Rowling's wild inventiveness: messenger owls, rooms and stairways at Hogwarts that change position during the night, elves with inferiority complexes, invisibility cloaks. Rowling's refusal to put a leash on her imagination helped make her one of the richest women in the world.

In case you're having difficulty giving your imagination free reign, here's a transitional ploy you can try: Conjure up a ghost story, a medical drama, or a western in which you reverse as many of the clichés associated with the genre that you can think of: a story about a ghost who is afraid of people; a female surgeon who becomes intimidated by her male colleagues; a cowboy who suffers from a fear of horses after being thrown from one. Each affliction sets up all sorts of conflict situations you will need to solve. What must the ghost do to overcome his fear of people and win the respect of his fellow ghosts? How does the female surgeon manage to perform successful operations if her fellow male surgeons try to discredit her techniques? How does the cowboy learn to overcome his trauma?

TAPPING INTO DREAMS

When you stop to think of it, all of us are natural-born storytellers in our dreams—daydreams as well as sleep dreams. I'm convinced that, even after more than a century of dream research (Sigmund Freud published his revolutionary *The Interpretation of Dreams* in 1900), there is more to learn about this extraordinary psychological phenomenon than we already know—and we do know a lot. In the opening paragraph of his famous book Freud asserted that not only is there a technique for interpreting dreams (which he devised), but that "every dream reveals itself as a psychical structure which has a meaning *and which can be inserted at an assignable point in the mental activities of waking life*" (emphasis added). Dreams, in other words, can be closely correlated with the dreamer's thoughts and activities when awake. Freud's disciple, Carl Jung, took this a step further by linking dreams to what he called the collective unconscious. Our dream symbolism is connected to the vast body of myth and legend. The symbolism in our dreams is universal, archetypal. These insights have considerable significance for writers: Dreams are a major resource for storytelling.

Many successful authors frequently tap into their dreams for ideas; for some of them dreams become central to their art. In *Writers Dreaming* (1993), Naomi Epel, a dream researcher, interviews twenty-six authors on how their dream lives inform their work. Clive Barker, for example, takes copious notes about what images are coming into his head and how they seem to be "rooted . . . in particular psycho-dramas of my own." Amy Tan explains that her writing is itself dream-like. "I focus on a specific image, and that image takes me into a scene. Then I begin to see the scene and I ask myself, 'What's to your right? What's to your left?' and I open up into this fictional world." Similarly, Stephen King states that part of his function as a writer "is to dream awake."

This is fascinating stuff to learn—but let's get practical: What particular techniques can you use to make your waking and sleeping dreams benefit your writing? Let's first consider daydreams, since they're easier to manage.

PRODUCTIVE DAYDREAMING

I know, that sounds like an oxymoron. We generally assume that day-dreaming is nonproductive by definition. But daydreaming puts the mind in an especially receptive mood for story ideas.

The first step is to get completely relaxed, but not drowsy. Recline in your favorite chair, but don't lie on the sofa or bed; you might fall asleep. Avoid distractions, except perhaps for soft daydream-enhancing music. Make sure your notebook and pencil are within arm's reach.

Next, let your thoughts wander. Don't force it—just go where your thoughts take you. Before long you will find yourself dwelling on one particular fantasy. It might feature casting for trout in a mountain lake or performing a famous role on the Broadway stage.

Finally, zero in on the fantasy to bring details into focus. This is where you need your notebook. Describe your daydream fantasy in a single sentence; then expand it into a paragraph; then into a two-page scenario, adding story ingredients (characters, incidents) as you go along.

NIGHTLY DREAMS AND HOW TO CAPTURE THEM

Some people keep dream journals on their nightstands. Because a dream fades so rapidly, you jot down as much of it as you can recall the moment you awaken. Some of what you recall may not make any sense, but record it anyway. The reason is that these surface non sequiturs or absurdities (what Freud called "manifest dream content") may have deeper significance.

Later, use your dream journal to work up a story premise. The stories themselves need not be "dreamlike" (although such stories are fascinating)—just unusual. Maybe you've dreamt that you were piloting a small aircraft, but suddenly forgot how to control the plane, and the next thing you recall is that you were trapped in a dark, windowless room. Possible story premise: Your narrator is the pilot of a spy plane that was shot down by the enemy and is now being held prisoner. Injuries he sustained in a crash landing have given him amnesia. As his memories slowly return, he remembers his mission and his training and figures out a way to escape.

FOR YOUR WRITER'S NOTEBOOK

1. Take ten blank sheets of loose-leaf notebook paper. At the top of each sheet write the name of a person you know: friends, relatives, co-workers, rivals. Over the next few hours, jot down as many details about each person as you can recall—physical

features, behavioral traits, pet peeves, favorite sayings, manner of dress, and so on. Don't invent anything; however, you can be hypothetical; e.g., "Jason seems sad most of the time." On the back of the sheet, conjure up a story idea that would be suitable for each person you describe; e.g., "Jason, who suffers from Seasonal Affective Disorder, meets a woman who has a similar affliction and together they find a way to overcome their affliction."

2. Choose a law or regulation you think is unjust (e.g., the maximum speed limit on freeways) and do the following:

   a. Explain why you think the law or regulation is unjust. Include your rebuttal of counterarguments that support it. Conduct necessary research to learn more about the law.

   b. Work up a story scenario in which your narrator struggles to do away with an unjust law (e.g., in the segregated South of the 1930s, a teacher dares to desegregate restaurants).

3. Write out a story idea based on one or more of the following "what if" questions.

   EXAMPLE: What if a terrorist group seized control of ICBMs armed with nuclear warheads? Story idea: Terrorist group demands a ransom of one trillion dollars from the U.S. government or else it will launch the missiles toward Washington, D.C., New York City, and Los Angeles.

   a. What if the Virgin Mary appeared at halftime during the Super Bowl?

   b. What if it became possible to genetically engineer specific abilities (athletic, artistic, and so forth) in fetuses?

   c. What if a homeless person won a one-hundred-million-dollar lottery? Or a neo-Nazi?

       d. What if someone invented a way to program the brain with new skills the way one programs a computer?

4. Let your imagination run wild (on paper) with one of the following prompts:

       a. Exploring a cave on the planet Mars

       b. A video game that hypnotizes its users long enough to give them posthypnotic suggestions

       c. Exploring an alien ocean (e.g., on Jupiter's moon Europa)

       d. An extinct million-year-old pathogen, revived in the lab, escapes confinement

       e. Archaeologists digging in the Negev Desert discover a new gospel

5. Keep a record of your daydreams for a single week. Write out a story idea for one or more of them.

6. Imagine a story in which the narrator discovers a trunk buried in the cellar of an abandoned house in New England. What is in the trunk? Who put it there, and why? When did this take place?

7. Record in a pocket notebook several story ideas that occur to you while you're visiting or attending a social function, such as a political campaign event or a wedding reception. Look for potential conflict situations that could form the basis of a story—e.g., an old flame of the bride or groom shows up at a wedding reception intent on causing trouble.

8. Dream up a fantasy scenario for a children's story, one in which you reverse the situation of an existing story. For example, a story about a Cinderella-like heroine with an evil fairy godmother and loving sisters.

CHAPTER 4

Working an Idea, Stage I:

FREE-ASSOCIATING

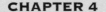

Blank pages inspire me with terror.

—MARGARET ATWOOD

Ideas for stories often are *sparked*—by a certain word you overhear, an unusual face you see on a crowded street, a memory-triggering sound such as a foghorn or siren. Even an everyday spectacle like a child roller-skating, geese in flight, an elderly couple strolling through a park, or bicyclists pumping their way up a steep road can awaken dormant memories and plant the seeds for stories. Experienced writers train themselves to capture such fleeting moments with a few jottings—let's not even call them sentences—that express a spontaneous train of association that the original stimulus has set into motion. These free association jottings are important because they can rapidly generate raw content for a story or essay. And even if they do not, practicing such free association can prove to be its own reward because such practice develops your ability to make fascinating connections between things you would not otherwise have considered relatable. To be able to free-associate productively, however, you need to turn off the editor inside your head, the one who wants you to think only relevant stay-inside-the-box thoughts.

OPENING THE FLOODGATES

We are all too often constrained by rules and regulations, mindful to a fault of what is considered acceptable or unacceptable language or behavior in a given social context. In school, many of us were taught (directly or indirectly) to be more attentive to the rules of grammar and punctuation than to the subjects we were writing about. No wonder creative expression often gets stifled, sometimes to a point beyond recovery. Free association, untethered by constraints, is one quick way to resuscitate creative thinking. Like an overstuffed closet, our long-term memories get cluttered. And just as it is likely to make surprising discoveries by sorting through that overstuffed closet, we can make some even more surprising discoveries by using free association to open the floodgates of memory.

As a matter of fact, the memory-as-overstuffed-closet metaphor can prove to be quite literal. Go ahead and unstuff one of your closets—or your attic or basement or even a junk drawer—and keep your notebook handy as your memory is shifted into high gear by old toys, schoolwork, clothing, vinyl recordings, documents, and correspondence. Reenvision yourself (or your relatives) at the time when any of these items were current. Jot down everything that comes to mind without any editing whatsoever—this is a time for remembering, not for shaping your prose style.

COAXING TACIT KNOWLEDGE TO THE SURFACE

You know a lot more than you think you know. Psychologists have shown that *tacit* knowledge—names, places, concepts, words embedded in the subconscious—greatly exceeds performance knowledge—that is, the knowledge we know we have and regularly put to use. The easiest way to prove this to yourself is to think of a subject you think you know *something* about and spend ten minutes or so writing down anything that comes to mind about that subject. Before long you will likely have filled a page with details about the subject. "Now how did I know all that?" is a common reaction. Given the right stimuli, we can quite deliberately "upgrade" our tacit knowledge to performance knowledge. That is to say, in order to make the most of the knowledge and experience you've accumulated throughout your life, you must first *gain access* to that knowledge and then *make creative use* of that knowledge—something professional writers do routinely. As the philosopher of science Michael Polanyi writes in one of his essays on tacit knowledge, "All human thought comes into existence by grasping the meaning and mastering the use of language" ("Tacit Knowing: Its Bearing on Some Problems of Philosophy," from *Knowing and Being: Essays by Michael Polanyi* [1969]).

CONNECTIONS, CONNECTIONS!

Not only do we know more than we realize, we also possess an innate ability to generate new insights by connecting one thought to another to another to another until we produce a vast web of interrelationships. Our brains are wired for this. It is part of what it means to be conscious, to make sense of the world, to be actively engaged with the world. Arthur Koestler, in his monumental study of creative thinking titled *The Act of Creation* (1964), points out that people often fall prey to "shallow rationalism," which leads us to repress our innate creativity. Conscious awareness, Koestler reminds us, "is a matter of degree. Conscious and unconscious experiences do not belong to different compartments of the mind; they form a continuous scale of gradations, of degrees of awareness." Moreover, in any act of creativity "there is an upward surge from some unknown, fertile, underground layers of the mind." Unless we make an effort to rid ourselves of shallow rationalism, our creative minds will atrophy from the absence of those upward surges of expression.

The first step, then, is to revitalize our powers of association. As natural as making connections is, we can always become better at it. Free-associating is a good way to do this—and besides, it's fun! As you form connections among seemingly random images or concepts, you're bound to experience delight and even amazement at how copious your associations can be. Go ahead, jot down any ten words or phrases that come to mind when you hear the word *getaway*. Perhaps your list looks something like this:

- wilderness
- secluded beach
- escape from stressful job
- fresh air
- binoculars
- mountains
- wide open spaces
- tranquility
- hiking
- spiritual replenishment

Almost at once you're able to conjure up an idea for a feature article, say, on how to plan for a weekend getaway in a mountain wilderness, or a meditative essay on how to follow Thoreau's footsteps in the twenty-first century, or how a wilderness vacation can revitalize your mind, your outlook on life, your job-related skills, and more. Or, if you're an aspiring novelist, you might work up a scenario in which, let's say, a war veteran suffering from post-traumatic stress disorder tries to heal his psychological wounds by retreating into the wilderness.

It may sound like a contradiction in terms, but it is possible to free-associate within predetermined parameters. The result is a more focused web of interconnections—quite useful when you want to generate in-depth information about, say, a particular character or a particular city (or particular section of a city) in which your story is set—details about her struggle to overcome sexist prejudices when she tried to compete in male-dominated sports like football or rugby, for example, or technical aspects of her profession. Is she a detective? Then you will need to convince your readers of her professional knowledge of detective work. A free association exercise can be immensely helpful: Jot down everything you already know about detective work, and very quickly you'll be keenly aware of the knowledge gaps you'll have to fill through research.

USING FREE ASSOCIATION TO GENERATE STORY CONTENT

Plotting a story can get fairly complicated, especially if you're working on a murder mystery or thriller. In Chapter 8 we will look closely at some of the ways in which a basic idea can be developed into a richly plotted story, full of the twists and turns that make commercial fiction so enjoyable. But it's never too early to think about plot, even at the idea-gathering free-association stage.

Let's return to that cluttered attic filled with forgotten family history. Imagine that you uncover a garment bag containing your grandfather's World War II service uniform.

Even the faintest notion of a story idea—(say he served as an Army soldier under General Wainwright during the battle for Corregidor) will suffice to begin free-associating within the parameters of that idea, this time moving from single words to phrases:

- Corregidor's battlefields, tunnels
- Japanese agenda for conquest
- bloodshed vs. surrender
- fighting beyond exhaustion
- capture; becoming a Japanese POW

- combat journal
- recurring nightmares of combat
- Grandfather's postwar trauma
- war's influence on his behavior, worldview

Free-associating can bring things to mind that could well prove to be of major importance later on, such as suddenly being reminded of the existence of a possible diary your grandfather might have kept chronicling the details of daily combat, a document that could even serve as the framing device of the story or novel you might eventually write.

Also, it is satisfying to discover all the possible connections we can come up with when we free-associate, even without any particular literary agenda. We merely want to comb our psyches for buried treasure. Sooner or later, however, we will want to use free association to generate raw material for a particular writing project.

It is one thing to feel strongly motivated to tell a particular story but quite another to be instantly aware of all that should be included in the telling. Some of the things you conjure up in your free-association lists will probably prove unusable, but it's likely that you would never have thought of these items had you plunged into a draft directly.

Even without a glimmer of a story idea, free association in itself can help you generate a wealth of potential story ideas. Different venues will help you produce different kinds of associations. We just considered one such venue: the battlefield. Here are several others.

THE AIRPORT

Airports are potentially excellent places for coming up with ideas for stories. I say *potentially* because most of the time our only goal is to get through check-in and security with our nerves intact, and if we're lucky, squeeze in enough time for a meal before boarding our 4-hour Peanut Express. But during those occasional interludes between mayhem and tedium, airports can serve us writers well by parading endless streams of diverse humanity before our eyes.

People watching in airports is a free-association exercise in action—and a good test of observational skills. Tactfully scope out individuals at random, or in selected places such as on trams or walkways or in restaurants, and pay close attention to their expressions, their clothing, the bags they have with them, the material they're reading, the food they're eating. Each of these details can suggest a story. Your observations, of course, may be totally wrong (you'll never know unless you strike up conversations with these individuals), but that's not the point. You are testing your ability to turn observations into ideas for stories.

THE LABORATORY

Not just the abode of mad scientists like Victor Frankenstein, Dr. Jekyll, or John Hammond (the dinosaur-breeding mastermind in Michael Crichton's *Jurassic Park*), the laboratory can be the source of some compelling dramas. Think of forensic labs where ballistic, DNA, or fingerprint analysis is conducted, or consider medical research labs where scientists closely examine the minutest phenomena in order to solve crimes—perhaps even those that were committed centuries or millennia ago (in this case the scientists examine mummies or fossilized remains). If you want to write a story about human space exploration, you probably should visit a NASA facility (such as the Ames Research Center in Mountain View, California) and tour, say, its hydroponics lab where experiments on growing crops without soil are being conducted. Free-associate about the possibilities of long-term spaceflights or colonizing the moon or Mars, where food must be "homegrown." Good science fiction ideas are extrapolated from solid scientific fact.

THE HOSPITAL

If airports show people in transition, hospitals show people in crisis. It is inside hospitals that we most keenly come face-to-face with our vulnerability, with our mortality, and also with our valiant and often successful efforts to overcome those limitations. Hospitals are full of story possibilities for those reasons.

Because most of us have either been hospitalized or have been with friends or family members who have been, we probably know more about the hospital scene than we realize. Free-associating on any hospital-related topic—nurse-patient relationships, ICU and E.R. procedures, surgeons making rounds, orderlies and volunteer workers going about their business, anxiety-filled visitors huddled together in waiting rooms—should prove fruitful in yielding a rich quantity of raw material.

If you are willing to volunteer your services (always valuable experience for a writer, not to mention a great humanitarian act), you might venture to a triage center where a disaster has occurred, such as a hurricane, flood, or explosion. Not only will you be observing medical professionals in dramatic emergency situations, you'll be participating through your assistance.

THE WORKPLACE

A third of our adult lives is spent, typically, in the service of our employers. For some that means commuting to an office, sales counter, factory, kitchen, or restaurant; for others, it means spending time on the road as a salesperson or consultant. Regardless of the nature of the work, or the places in which the work is performed, there is much raw material for stories to be found on the job. You say that your office job is too humdrum for story material? Did you ever see the 1980 movie *Nine to Five*? Three women (played by Jane Fonda, Dolly Parton, and Lily Tomlin), incarcerate their sexist-pig boss (played by Dabney Coleman), and take over the company's production. Every workplace is a treasure trove of potential stories, but you need to brainstorm for possibilities. Begin by free-associating about some of the things that can happen during the day in the life of, say, a bank teller, or an interviewer at an employment agency, or a clerk in a department store's complaint department.

THE WILDERNESS

Memorable stories, essays, and memoirs of pilgrimage or enlightenment are set in a wilderness of one sort or another. Take, for instance,

marms alone; we overedit because we're afraid of stepping over the line, of saying something dumb. But we overlook one simple fact: When you're free-associating, or even writing a first draft, you are writing for your eyes only. Proofreading is for getting a final draft ready for print; only then does it make sense to worry about grammar and punctuation. "The habit of compulsive, premature editing," asserts English professor Peter Elbow in his landmark book *Writing without Teachers* (1973), "doesn't just make writing hard. It also makes writing dead. Your voice is damped out by all the interruptions, changes, and hesitations between the consciousness and the page."

Free-associating on paper may seem like junk writing, and in a sense it is: You're not writing for an audience, nor are you even writing for yourself. Instead you're writing to break through the shell of restraint, of fear, of uncertainty that has kept many a would-be writer from becoming a published author. The blank page is frightening, but if you're really a writer at heart, you're going to be *inspired* by that terror, as Margaret Atwood expresses it (see the epigraph to this chapter). Inspired? Yes, because that empty page is telling you that you have the resources to do it.

And there may be a few gold nuggets in that junk writing—raw stuff you've brought up from the dregs of your subconscious.

FOR YOUR WRITER'S NOTEBOOK

1. Take out a sheet of notebook paper and jot down whatever five to ten words come to mind. Next, choose one of these words—the word that you sense can best spark an idea for a story—and jot down five words or phrases you instantly associate with that word. Finally, reshape what you've written into a synopsis for a short story.

2. The next time you find yourself inside an airport terminal, describe two or three of the people sitting next to you. Next, cre-

ate an imaginary profile for each of them. If you feel comfortable doing so, initiate a conversation with one of these persons in order to come up with additional details.

3. Do some free-associating for a "ship of fools" story. You might imagine a spectrum of characters with very different backgrounds, personalities, and agendas headed for a common destination, unaware of certain dangers awaiting them. Or, if you have a yen for supernatural horror, free-associate about a ship taken over by ghosts who, say, decide to work together to terrorize a port city. Don't worry about plot points at this stage; your first goal is to generate possible content.

4. Visit a hospital and familiarize yourself with the particular kinds of care that nurses provide patients, including routine procedures such as catheterization or monitoring of vital signs. Also pay attention to hospital ambiance (sounds, smells, décor) and, of course, the appearances and attitudes of patients in a given ward. Later, spend a half hour or so free-associating about hospitals.

5. Do some free-associating about amusement park attractions, like wild rides, fun house mirrors, haunted houses, dioramas, costumed characters, live performances, and so on.

6. Interview a homeless person or persons. Later, free-associate to generate possible scenarios in which a homeless person makes a strange discovery that changes his or her life.

7. Brainstorm about a day in the life of a department store employee who hears complaints for a living. What kinds of strange complaints can you imagine coming his or her way?

8. Imagine a street vendor who sells magical toys. What kinds of toys are they? What magic are they capable of? What kind of person is the vendor, and how did he or she come by these toys?

CHAPTER 5

Working an Idea, Stage II:

LISTING, MAPPING, PROFILING, AND ILLUSTRATING WITH COLLAGES

A writer is someone on whom nothing is lost. —**HENRY JAMES**

Free association, as we have seen in the previous chapter, is an excellent way to stimulate your brain into generating a lot of raw material that can be screened for story ideas. But before plunging into a draft or even an outline, you may find it worthwhile to produce more detailed content based on the story idea you wish to develop. Having come up with more details than you need is preferable to not having enough details. Even though you're not concerned with plotting just yet (that will come shortly), by generating raw details related to circumstance, setting, and characters, you will be in a better position to plot your story. This chapter will guide you through several content-generating pre-drafting activities that will better prepare you for the more complex tasks of plotting and drafting: listing, mapping, character profiling, and illustrating with collages.

THE USEFULNESS OF PRE-DRAFTING ACTIVITIES

Lists, maps, profiles, and collages are pre-drafting tools that can help you lay the groundwork for a story. They are more structured than free association, but less structured than outlines or synopses. Lists will provide you with an inventory of story content; maps will help you determine a basic layout of story events; profiles will give you a better sense of how to delineate the individuals in your story; and collages will help you visualize the story. Although it is not necessary to undertake these tasks in the order presented, doing so does follow a logical progression of increasing complexity. The point is to be flexible. You may feel the need to do two or more simultaneously, or recursively (that is, start with some character profiling, then turn to listing, then go back to some basic free-associating, then do more listing, and so on). In fact, some writers begin drafting *before* engaging in a content-generating prewriting task such as listing or mapping.

THE ART OF LISTING

I mention listing first because it's the easiest, and we do it all the time, even to help ourselves fall asleep (itemizing the events of the previous day or the tasks we must complete at work the next day or the things we need to buy during tomorrow's shopping trip). Because a list presupposes a category for the items listed, your first task is to come up with promising categories—ones under which you could list lots of things. Start with easy categories. If you're working on a memoir, then think childhood-related categories:

- Fears
- Fun and games

- Mishaps
- Earliest school memories
- Buddies and bullies
- Foods you loved; foods you hated
- Favorite bedtime stories
- Toys
- Earliest school memories (kindergarten through fourth grade)
- Pets
- Tough lessons learned the hard way

The items you list will not only help you recall old memories, they will remind you of details that have long since faded away. Writers need to draw from every aspect and every moment of their lives when creating characters. Everything stems from the self.

Planning to take a trip? It's always a good idea to keep a travel diary; but along with your conventional entries—accounts of your day-to-day adventures—list the names (along with brief descriptions) of people you've met, unusual customs, of favorite paintings and other museum exhibits, of unusual meals and landmarks. Lists have a way of triggering entire experiences; at the very least, they will reduce the likelihood of forgetting so-called minor details or incidents, details that can help add verisimilitude to a story.

Let's say that you are visiting a tropical rain forest. Perhaps you would like to write a personal-experience essay or a short story based on a memorable rain forest revelation. A good place to begin would be to draw up several lists, each relating to some facet of the rain forest you visited. Some of your lists might be categorized by country (rain forests of Costa Rica, of Brazil, of Trinidad); some of your lists might be limited to rain forest vegetation (trees, flowers, herbs, grasses, fruits, vines)—and any of those items can trigger their own lists (different species and uses of medicinal herbs; herbs used in cooking; dangerous herbs), and of course animal life, with each genus or species of animal being given its own list—monkeys, snakes, spiders, ants, and so on.

Keep in mind that the purpose of these lists is to provide you with an inventory of details you may need to have at your fingertips should you decide to write, say, a short story about a botanist who tries to prevent the destruction of a section of rain forest that may harbor a very rare medicinal herb that could help cure Alzheimer's; or a profile of a Jane Goodall-like primatologist who has been working hard to keep a rare species of monkey from going extinct. To write pieces like that you want to become as much of an expert in herbs and their pharmacological possibilities or monkeys and the importance of preserving their native habitats. The lists you draw up will serve as a starting point for further research.

Every item on your lists has the potential to become a bona fide idea in itself. In a list of rainforest birds, for example, you might suddenly find yourself getting an idea for a children's story about one of the exotic birds—a parrot, toucan, ibis, flamingo, or hummingbird, let's say. For that particular species of bird, you would then prepare a list of attributes, physical and behavioral, that account for its distinctiveness.

Also, you may already have discovered that every item on your lists can become a header for a subsidiary list. Make *parrot* the header for a new list and you might list parrot species, parrots as pets, parrots in literature and art, parrots and pirates, parrots that speak, and so on. You can also list ideas that relate to speaking parrots, some of which could be fashioned into a story, others of which could be incorporated into a story. For example:

PARROTS THAT SPEAK
- Best ways of training a parrot to speak
- How parrots vocalize words
- Children's story about a speaking parrot whose vocalizations get him into trouble
- Mystery story about a parrot that witnesses a crime and identifies the culprit by name
- Story about a philosopher parrot

- Story about a mischievous parrot that is taught to use a cell phone

FROM LISTING TO MAPPING

Once you have filled several pages with lists based on your categories, you are ready to connect some of the dots—to map out relationships among the individual items. This should prove to be easier than it at first seems because we instinctively make connections among things that are not already connected in some way. A psychologist would say that it is human nature to make connections, to perceive shapes in shapeless formations, to determine patterns. The ancients, gazing up at the night sky, discerned patterns among the stars (we call those patterns constellations); and in different cultures different patterns were discerned: some saw a dipper, others a bear; still others an oxcart. At times we go overboard in our pattern seeking, detecting the faces of saints in coffee grounds and that sort of thing. But for the most part, the ability to detect patterns—to find order in the chaos—is important.

To see how mapping works, let's return to our idea for a children's story based upon a parrot. After perusing the lists we made for the various species, we decide to map out a story idea about a parrot that not only has mastered human speech, but has become a trickster figure, one who creates mischief just for the heck of it. What can we map out about our mischievous parrot that would give us enough material for a story? Quite a lot! In fact, we can say so much that we would need not one type of mapping strategy but two: analysis mapping and action mapping.

ANALYSIS MAPPING

With an analysis map your aim is to be able to easily scrutinize your subject from all sides, as it were. Using our loquacious hero as a case in point, we might produce the following fact sheets about our parrot, whom we'll name Charlene. Our analysis map might look like this:

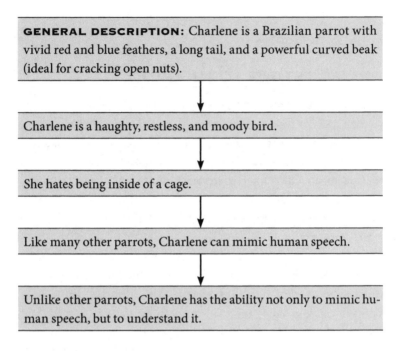

GENERAL DESCRIPTION: Charlene is a Brazilian parrot with vivid red and blue feathers, a long tail, and a powerful curved beak (ideal for cracking open nuts).

Charlene is a haughty, restless, and moody bird.

She hates being inside of a cage.

Like many other parrots, Charlene can mimic human speech.

Unlike other parrots, Charlene has the ability not only to mimic human speech, but to understand it.

ACTION MAPPING

Use an action map to establish causal relationships between one event and another in the story you're planning to write. For our children's story in progress about Charlene the talking parrot, we might map out the action as follows:

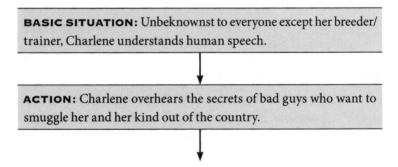

BASIC SITUATION: Unbeknownst to everyone except her breeder/trainer, Charlene understands human speech.

ACTION: Charlene overhears the secrets of bad guys who want to smuggle her and her kind out of the country.

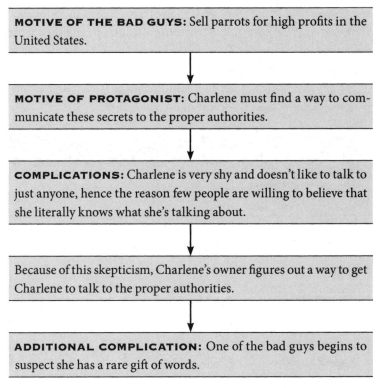

MOTIVE OF THE BAD GUYS: Sell parrots for high profits in the United States.

MOTIVE OF PROTAGONIST: Charlene must find a way to communicate these secrets to the proper authorities.

COMPLICATIONS: Charlene is very shy and doesn't like to talk to just anyone, hence the reason few people are willing to believe that she literally knows what she's talking about.

Because of this skepticism, Charlene's owner figures out a way to get Charlene to talk to the proper authorities.

ADDITIONAL COMPLICATION: One of the bad guys begins to suspect she has a rare gift of words.

These mapping strategies will give you both the content and the overall design of your developing story idea, so that when you turn to the more demanding task of outlining the story, you will be less likely to falter.

DEVELOPING CHARACTERS THROUGH PROFILING

There are at least two ways to profile your characters: by preparing a data sheet for each of them and by writing conventional prose descriptions. I recommend doing both. The data sheet is another type of listing, and you can set up the criteria ahead of time. The prose description enables you to weave your character into the fabric of the narrative more easily. It makes sense first to prepare a data sheet for each character in your story, take a few days to modify it, and then write out a page of conventional description in which you integrate the attributes listed on your data sheet.

To get started, prepare a data sheet template. Here is an example (you may want to modify it for your own purposes):

CHARACTER DATA SHEET

Full name of character _____

Age, gender _____

Ethnicity _____

Religious orientation _____

Sexual orientation _____

Marital status _____

Physical description
    a. Facial details _____
    _____

    b. Height, weight _____
    c. Body type _____
    _____

Behavioral characteristics
    a. General temperament (moody, easygoing, neurotic, other) _____
    _____

    b. Noticeable eccentricities, tics _____
    _____

    c. Type of voice (screechy, whining, gruff, sonorous, other) _____
    _____

d. Speech habits (e.g., stutters, says "uhm" or "you know" a lot) _____

_____

Education _____

Occupation(s) _____

_____

Ambition(s), dreams _____

_____

Favorite foods, drinks _____

_____

Favorite clothes _____

_____

Biggest accomplishments _____

_____

Most serious flaws, fears, or phobias _____

_____

Most serious mistakes _____

_____

Role in the story (novel, memoir) being planned:

a. Goal in the story _____

_____

b. Underlying motive(s) _____

_____

c. Obstacles he or she faces _____

_____

d. Tentative plans for overcoming the obstacles _____

_____

The purpose behind preparing data sheets for your characters is to generate ideas about how they may come across in your story. It really doesn't matter how much of this data you incorporate; it may turn out that you don't use any of it, but spontaneously come up with new attributes during the drafting stage. By completing character profiles you will be more likely to regard your characters as real persons and render them realistically in your stories, whether or not you make overt use of the attributes you have listed.

The next step in character profiling is to write up a one-page description for each character, incorporating their respective attributes from the data sheets. You may handle this in one of two ways:

1. A straightforward descriptive summary
2. A narrative rendering, as if it were actually a part of your story

Here is an example of a descriptive summary, using the first-person narrator in Poe's tale "The Facts in the Case of M. Valdemar" as a case in point:

Poe's narrator (referred to only as "P—") is a specialist in the art of mesmerism (hypnotism) who, through his commitment to the facts, in his highly serious demeanor, and in his professional treatment of Ernest Valdemar (the patient in question) comes across as highly skilled and highly rational. These attributes make his decision to hypnotize Valdemar into reporting his sensations at the very moment of his death seem all the more believable.

And here is how Poe renders dramatically one facet of the narrator's behavior that I have summarized:

> When [my colleagues] had gone, I spoke freely with M. Valdemar on the subject of his approaching dissolution, as well as . . . the experiment proposed. He still professed himself quite willing and even anxious to have it made, and urged me to commence it at once. A male and a female nurse were in attendance, but I did not feel myself altogether at liberty to

engage in a task of this character with no more reliable
witnesses than these people, in case of sudden accident,
might prove. I therefore postponed operations until about
eight the next night, when the arrival of a medical student
with whom I had some acquaintance relieved me from far-
ther embarrassment.

Here we see Poe showing dramatically what I have summarized ab-
stractly. The realistic, dramatic rendering of an idea about a character is one of the most important skills for writers to acquire, one that
takes considerable practice.

ILLUSTRATING YOUR
STORY IDEA WITH COLLAGES

We live in a visual age, and with good reason. As the poet-naturalist
Diane Ackerman explains in *A Natural History of the Senses* (1990),
"Our eyes are the great monopolists of our senses . . . Our language is
steeped in visual imagery." Using visuals of all sorts, from photographs
to drawings (our own or those clipped from periodicals) stimulates
right-brain perception, that is, helps us to perceive our abstract ideas
physically, three-dimensionally.

Of course, you can illustrate your story ideas with original drawings or paintings; but because many writers are not trained in those
techniques of illustration, an excellent alternative is to employ pre-
existing images (or scraps of images) in an original manner.

To make collages, all you need are old magazines, newspapers, scissors, and paste. You may also add original drawings to the collage, using pastels, watercolors, or other media.

The idea here is to capture visually what you intend to convey ver-
bally in your story. Think about how you might illustrate the story of
a talking parrot. You might include a large magazine photograph of a
colorful parrot and then surround the bird with smaller images that
relate to speech or speech communication.

71

FOR YOUR WRITER'S NOTEBOOK

1. Imagine that you have been asked to write a narrative (fiction or nonfiction) about a site of historical, cultural, or industrial interest that you have visited recently (a factory, museum, state fair, antiques show, arts and crafts studio, or war memorial). Prepare a list of details observed at that site.

2. Prepare an analysis and/or action map based on the site for which you've prepared a list.

3. Using the list and map(s) you prepared for exercises 1 and 2, draw up a data sheet for at least two individuals who are associated with the site you visited.

4. Using clippings from old magazines and newspapers, create a collage that would illustrate a representative scene from a story or personal-experience essay you would like to write.

5. Create a story map based on one or more of the following ideas:
   a. A detective searches for a serial killer whom everyone assumed to have died ten years ago but is once again leaving telltale signs of his or her presence
   b. A children's story in which a leprechaun, scorned by his fellow leprechauns for being too tall, decides he wants to try his luck among ordinary people
   c. A *Twilight Zone*–type of story about a woman who unknowingly meets her future self in an airport terminal. What does her future self warn her about? How does her present self react? What are the consequences?

6. Make a collage that would illustrate the story you mapped in the previous exercise.

7. After reading Poe's "The Facts in the Case of M. Valdemar" (available online), prepare a data sheet for M. Valdemar, using only details that Poe himself provides. Which attributes listed

on the data sheet are not mentioned or inferred in the story? How useful would they be if Poe had included them?

8. Write a comprehensive one-page summary of M. Valdemar based on Poe's rendering.

9. Create character data sheets for each of the following:

   a. A brilliant scientist who suffers from a debilitating phobia

   b. An ex-convict trying to fit into society

   c. The wildly eccentric CEO of a toy factory

CHAPTER 6

Working an Idea, Stage III:

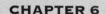

PREPARING AN OUTLINE AND SYNOPSIS

As much as it might seem like a potential killjoy, many writers ... find outlines absolutely indispensable.

—DAVID HARRIS EBENBACH

If you have been following the chapters in this book in sequence, by now you have mined your original idea for enough material to begin *working* that idea—that is, crafting a novel or personal-experience narrative. Some writers will say that the toughest work is behind you. After all, for the past month or so you've been filling dozens of pages with possible ideas, free associations triggered by the most promising of those ideas, lists filled with information about story settings and situations, character profiles, outlines, and maps of the story terrain to help you envision your story's themes and structure. In this chapter and the chapters that follow—writing a synopsis; sculpting the story structure; drafting the narrative itself; and revising the draft—you should be able to proceed rapidly toward your long-anticipated goal of finishing a novel or memoir. Be pleased with what you have accomplished thus far: You have conjured up a story idea. You have also built up that idea by observing things keenly, or by conjuring things up out of the blue, thanks to your enhanced cognitive skills. Are you working with your idea for a novel? (We'll get to memoirs later in this chapter.) Now it is time for you to begin working out the details of a plotline suggested by that idea.

"Plotline"? What is that?

Very simply, it is the sinuous path along which your story idea unfolds as it moves through an obstacle course (if you're writing a thriller, that obstacle course might best be characterized as a minefield), toward the climactic moment when the conflict gets resolved. Around every bend, someone or something will appear either to help or to hinder your protagonist's progress. In the best stories the hindrances will seem unbeatable until the very end. Think of the yellow brick road that Dorothy must follow if she is to reach the Wizard in the Emerald City. Everything that happens along this road—rescuing the Scarecrow, the Tin Woodman, and the Cowardly Lion; meeting the Guardian of the Gates—is a plot point, a subsidiary idea that must connect meaningfully to the main idea. In an outline all you need to do is mention (and maybe briefly describe) each plot point leading to the climax of the story (the confrontation with the Wizard) and the conclusion (Dorothy's return home).

Right now you're probably saying, Whoa! Slow down! How do I get from idea (or even the mapping and freewriting I generated based on that idea) to a plotline consisting of several subsidiary ideas? Well, take a closer look at your main idea: The seeds for the subsidiary ideas are already there. All you need to do is tease them out and flush them into the open by questioning the implications: If this happens, or doesn't happen, then what? Thus you will convert potentiality into actuality, into explicit movement.

Also think about your viewpoint character: How should this person move from point A to point B to point C in order to reach his or her goal? Just as you were inventive in developing your idea, you have to continue being inventive when you're working out the plot details. It can be fun but also scary because there will be occasions when your story goes slack or goes off on a tangent or starts to feel contrived—or when your protagonist somehow manages to back herself into a corner. What then? You simply backtrack: You retrace your steps until you pinpoint the fork in the road and let your character embark on a more promising direction. Here's where outlining can be a great help.

THE PRACTICALITY OF OUTLINES

There was a time when I cringed at the very word *outline*. It brought back grim memories of militant English teachers who made the act of writing essays (usually referred to as "themes") seem like drudgery, sometimes even punishment. ("Fred, you will stay after school and write a five-hundred-word theme on why it's bad manners to pull girls' ponytails.") Themes had to be preceded by a mandatory outline, which was then covered with corrections (in red ink, of course), and branded with a grade, usually low enough to destroy any remaining motivation for writing the essay, and possibly for writing anything again the rest of your life. Why were so many teachers distrustful of fostering creative expression? Maybe it was because creativity seemed disorderly, unpredictable, difficult if not impossible to measure, hence to grade. Maybe, too, because creative expression smacked of rebellion, resisting authority and convention, a tendency to disregard or stretch the rules. Except that creative thinking, especially as it is manifested in creative writing, doesn't do away with rules so much as reinterpret them—but only when there's a valid reason for doing so. I like to think of outlines as a practical way of spurring both creative thinking and logical thinking (one always needs both, in varying degrees, when writing fiction and non-fiction). Just as painters create "studies"—quick, miniature versions of the larger painting they want to execute—so do novelists and memoirists lay out the basic plan of their work with an outline and/or synopsis.

OUTLINING AS IDEA PROMPTING

Like creative writing in general, outlining, contrary to common, schoolmarm-bred assumptions, is not rule bound. It is a heuristic device—a means of generating ideas relating to story content—flexible enough to be adaptable as the novel or memoir evolves. Outlines work best when they are flexible; they have to be because as the original story idea develops into a multifaceted interplay of actions and reactions, the outline can serve as a beacon for what should come next.

Not all writers work with outlines; no one says you have to. Plenty of writers begin drafting as soon as an idea strikes them, no matter how nebulous that idea is—they relish the sensation of wondering what will pop into their heads next. They say it makes drafting more pleasurable than if they know the entire structure ahead of time. Some writers wait until they finish drafting a couple chapters before they work up an outline, at which time the story idea will have become more focused, the direction in which the story should go more discernible. Do what works best for you. That said, if you haven't yet tried your hand at outlining, I strongly recommend that you do so to see if it suits you. Likelier than not, it will. As David Ebenbach, a member of the Gotham Writers Workshop faculty, asserts, "Outlines work because they allow writers to distill their amorphous creations into their crucial parts, to find the places where tension will need to be increased and the place, or places, where crisis will set in and climax will result."

TYPES OF OUTLINES

Consider the different types of outlines you can use to begin structuring your story ideas:

SCRATCH OUTLINES

You've probably outlined without even realizing it: an idea for a story strikes you while you're having lunch. If you're like me, ideas come to you anytime, anyplace. For some reason, I get ideas in restaurants. When that happens, I either pull out my pocket notebook (assuming I remembered to bring it) or grab a napkin and jot down something like this:

> Story about a real estate speculator who strikes it rich during housing bubble
>> —becomes overconfident in his investments.
>> —goes bust when housing market collapses in 2008
>> —resorts to fraudulent schemes to recoup his losses

That's one kind of scratch outline—pretty bare bones; but after all, I could be lunching with a friend and do not want to be rude by suddenly outlining a story idea.

When you aren't too busy at your day job or lunching with a friend, you might prepare a somewhat more detailed scratch outline:

> Story premise: Respected banker blackmailed into giving robber access to the bank vault.

Hmmm . . . not bad, you think; but how will you build a story out of that? Scratch outline to the rescue:

I. Robber threatens to report banker's embezzlement from years back unless he assists in the robbery.
II. Backstory: Desperate to make ends meet, banker embezzled money from the bank; wife found out about it.
III. Banker and wife separate after wife gets romantically involved with bank robber, tells him about banker's transgression.
IV. Just before the robbery takes place, banker confesses his embezzlement; in exchange for pardon, he will risk his life thwarting the robbers. Bank president agrees.

    V. Robbery gets underway; undercover police intervene—but not before robber shoots banker.

    VI. Banker survives; robber hauled off to jail.

Each statement represents a principal part of the story—the opening predicament, the strong opposition, the climactic event, the resolution.

FORMAL OUTLINES

Later on, as the idea begins to take shape, you may want to work up that scratch outline by adding specific details, a more explicit unfolding of events, and a clearer relationship between major plot points and what they consist of. For example:

    I. Robber threatens to report banker's embezzlement from years back unless he assists in the robbery.

        a. Robber (Joe) and banker (Clarence) were once co-workers at the bank.

        b. They had actually been good friends, but the friendship ended after Clarence betrayed Joe by telling Joe's girlfriend that he (Joe) had once been arrested for petty theft.

        c. Joe gets even by telling Clarence's wife that her husband is cheating on her.

. . . and so on. You are now on your way toward producing a formal outline, one you can use as a template while drafting (see Chapter 8).

PREPARING A PLOT OUTLINE PAINLESSLY

In any story, whether fiction or nonfiction, things happen—that's what makes them stories. These happenings need not be action scenes like car chases or explosions; misplacing a house key could well suffice as a happening—a plot point—because of the future happenings that result from it. For example, the time your narrator takes to locate the missing key causes her to miss the interview that would have resulted in a stagnating job; as a result she winds up landing a job that brings her international fame and fortune.

An event can even be internal, such as your narrator's sudden insight into a problem. A story will contain many events; but for the sake of preparing an outline, you want to pinpoint those events that move the story ever closer to the climax.

A good way to get an outline going is to keep asking questions about your story idea. *What needs to happen next?* That's your key question (assuming you've settled on a solid story idea; if not, you need to leap a few squares back to free-associating, brainstorming, and mapping (Chapters 2 and 3). This is yet another example of how any story idea really consists of dozens, maybe even hundreds, of subordinate ideas, all of which must add up to a coherent whole.

One of the reasons you may not be too enamored of outlines is that your grade-school teachers insisted you adhere to a fixed form. Of course, you can structure your outline any way you wish: You're preparing it for your eyes only, after all. On the other hand, if you haven't used an outline before, a template can help a lot. Try it, and if it doesn't work for you, modify it until it does—or do away with it altogether.

Here is a template. See if you can use it to your advantage.

OUTLINE TEMPLATE

Story Title (tentative): _____

Story Premise (one sentence): _____

_____

_____

_____

_____

Segment I: Conflict situation (protagonist's goal vs. antagonist's goal): ____

_____

_____

Segment II: Backstory; underlying problem leading up to the present situation: _____

_____

_____

_____

Segment III: Unfolding of the present circumstance leading to climax (showdown; revelation): _____

_____

_____

_____

Segment IV: Resolution, consequences of the final showdown or revelation:

_____

_____

_____

STORYBOARDING

A good outline will give you the handle you need to transform your story idea into a full-fledged narrative. Some writers will jump from outline into first draft, but I recommend working out your story's progress more fully by using a long-standing technique of Hollywood scriptwriters called "storyboarding."

Years ago I visited Rowan Oak, the antebellum home of William Faulkner in Oxford, Mississippi. One of America's greatest novelists, Faulkner told haunting stories of the lives of Southerners, stories intertwined with heroic as well as infamous family histories, often conveyed through interior monologue and sumptuous descriptions. If you're familiar with any of Faulkner's works, you may be surprised to learn that he was lured by Hollywood and actually spent time in Hollywood working on scripts. He was an unlikely candidate for Hollywood-style success, if there ever was one. After one such experience, he rushed back to Mississippi and never returned to Hollywood. However, he liked the storyboarding technique he learned while in Hollywood and used it to map out one of his novels. Here's the weird part: He storyboarded directly onto the walls of his study. No, he didn't tape index cards or butcher paper to the walls; he wrote directly onto the walls! It is quite a sight to behold.

I'm certainly not implying that you write out the scenes of your story directly onto the walls of your home—I shared the Faulkner story because it rather amusingly illustrates just how infectious a habit storyboarding can become. I recommend, instead, investing in a couple large corkboards and tacking storyboard cards to them. Then you can arrange the cards in sequences that instantly show the progression of events.

Here is why: Being a visually oriented species, we will have an easier time conceptualizing scenes, whether scenes for a movie or scenes for a novel, if we sketch them out on cards or sheets of paper. In fact, it would be most helpful to accompany your scene descriptions with drawings, and no, you don't have to be Rembrandt to produce useful sketches that go a long way toward helping you visualize the settings and situations comprising your plot.

Take a look at a storyboard series for a short story in which the narrator experiences a religious awakening while visiting the Vatican.

Narrator entering St. Peter's Basilica for the first time; at first is put off by the crowd.

Then he finds himself standing before Michelangelo's *Pieta* and is overwhelmed by its sublime beauty, despite its protective enclosure.

↓

A woman standing next to him recalls the time when a vandal attacked the sculpture with a hammer (the event leading to the protective casing).

↓

Narrator and the woman continue exploring St. Peter's together; she weaves anecdotes about the history of the basilica with those from her own life.

↓

Narrator realizes that the woman is strangely intensifying his spiritual feelings with each story she tells.

↓

When they go down to the lower level to see the crypts of several popes, she tells the narrator an especially haunting story.

↓

Things become complicated for the narrator, who is married (but separated), when he begins experiencing a powerful romantic attraction to the woman.

TRANSFORMING A PLOT OUTLINE INTO A PLOT SYNOPSIS

The nice thing about outlining is that you can postpone concerns about transitional elements—moving smoothly from situation A to situation B to situation C and so on. Your exclusive concern at the outline stage is story content; that is, the situations themselves. What do you want them to be? The question is a complex one; obviously you do not want to invent situations arbitrarily. Each situation must fulfill several objectives at once:

1. It must move the story closer to, or further away from, the protagonist's objective.
2. It must be intrinsically engrossing.
3. It should be both inevitable and surprising: inevitable in that readers understand that the protagonist is obliged to enter a minefield of danger; surprising in the particular kind of danger she faces.
4. It should reveal a new aspect of the protagonist's nature or reinforce an established one.

These situations together must make for a coherent string of events. Turning your outline into a synopsis will help you to ensure that coherence. A good synopsis will not only summarize the key elements of your story (an outline can do that too), but present in concentrated form the movement of one event to the next. This is an important step, especially if you have had little experience with drafting a narrative. Think of a synopsis as the succinct, easy-to-follow answer to the question, "How does your story unfold from beginning to end?"

Keep in mind that you may find yourself preparing two synopses: one for yourself and one that you may eventually submit to a potential agent or editor.

The synopsis you prepare for yourself should be as detailed as possible—nearly a draft, but without full dramatic rendering. In the case of a novel synopsis, that means covering every event in every chapter. Such a detailed synopsis (which can run as long as twenty or thirty pages) will be your blueprint for the first draft.

The synopsis you submit to an agent or editor will be much shorter, focusing only on the most important incidents. This synopsis will be more like a detailed summary. Its purpose is to help the agent or editor reach a decision as quickly as possible regarding the marketability of the proposed novel or memoir.

Let's begin with the long synopsis, the one you will prepare for yourself as a blueprint for your first draft. I like to think of this kind of synopsis as *sculpting* the story structure—paying close attention to every movement of the plot as it carves its way from opening predicament to middle complication to concluding climax and resolution.

Five elements should be present in your synopsis:

1. A clear understanding of your protagonist's desires and/or needs
2. A sense of the possible consequences of success or failure
3. A clear articulation of the obstacles, of the antagonist(s)' desires and needs
4. The solution to the conflict, however foolhardy or clever enough to overcome the perceived obstacles
5. The outcome

Note how these five elements appear in the following synopsis, from *Benet's Reader's Encyclopedia*, 3rd Edition, of *Things Fall Apart* (1958) by the distinguished Nigerian novelist Chinua Achebe (b. 1930):

> Set in eastern Nigeria during the British expansion into Igboland, the novel recounts the tragedy of Okonkwo and his clansmen under British colonialism. When Okonkwo, a respected tribal leader, accidentally kills one of his clansmen, he is banished from his village for seven years. On his return, he finds his village subject to colonial laws and his tribal beliefs replaced by Christianity. Okonkwo opposes these new practices but finds the villagers divided. In a moment of rage, he kills a messenger from the British District Officer, only to find that his clansmen will not support him. He hangs himself in despair.

This, of course, is what might be called a skeletal synopsis (sort of equivalent to a scratch outline). You may find it useful to prepare an extended chapter-by-chapter synopsis. Here, for example, is my synopsis of Chapter One of Achebe's novel:

> The story opens with an introduction to the hero, Okonkwo, and his deceased father, Unoka. Okonkwo proved his warrior skills by defeating a great wrestler known as Amalinze the Cat; however, Okonkwo's father, Unoka, although a high-spirited musician in his youth, became lazy and impoverished. Because his father died a failure and heavily in debt, Okonkwo was ashamed of him. Nevertheless, Okonkwo made it clear to the villagers that he deserved to be taken on his own merits, and that he would be destined for great things.

SCULPTING THE STORY STRUCTURE IN AN EXTENDED SYNOPSIS

It's a little scary, this story sculpting. What may have seemed like a simple idea for a story at the conceptual stage, or even at the outlining or synopsis stage, may now seem a lot more daunting. That's because you have arrived at a stage in planning where you must micromanage your characters; that is, you must oversee their actions with a sharp eye, making sure everyone behaves realistically and consistently according to the distinctive personalities and objectives you've provided them with.

It is also time to think about *pacing*, the time frame in which the story events unfold, from moment to moment as well as from day to day. It's not unlike blocking a stage play as rehearsals get underway. If you're working on a novel, you also have to keep track of the separate yet integral story lines and viewpoints, and ensure that they all come together properly. Not surprisingly, you may be tempted to skip this sculpting stage and leap directly into a first draft, but the sculpting will help ensure a plot structure that will not collapse on you halfway into your story. As you can see, writing at this stage is very different from writing at the idea-developing stage.

A forewarning: As you begin sculpting your story, you are likely to encounter unexpected obstacles, plot twists and turns that are arbitrary or contrived, and background information you've over-looked during your preliminary research. Ideas inevitably beget other ideas, after all. The most experienced storytellers grapple with such unexpected hurdles, so don't let it frustrate you. Writers will even revamp their entire outline—which is a better idea than plunging into the draft and reaching a dead end after a hundred pages.

BECOMING MINDFUL OF READERS' STORY EXPECTATIONS

Readers will expect the story to answer five questions:

1. Why do your protagonist's actions matter?
2. To what extraordinary lengths must your protagonist go to achieve her worthy objectives, and why?
3. What extraordinary resistance will the opposition produce in an effort to stop your protagonist, and why?
4. What are the consequences of failure for both protagonist and antagonist?
5. Will this story unfold in a way that keeps me turning the pages, forgetting that I'm reading a book but making me feel I'm experiencing an adventure?

Let's consider each of these questions a bit further, for answering them satisfactorily will ensure that your story ideas become successful stories.

Why do your protagonist's actions matter?

Your protagonist's actions not only must matter, they must matter a great deal—not necessarily a life-or-death matter, but close to it: Her happiness (sanity, fortune, family, or such) is at stake. Without the imminent possibility of a major gain, or major loss, of some kind, you don't have a story.

To what lengths must your protagonist go to achieve her worthy objectives, and why?

What must your protagonist do, specifically, to get what she wants? The greater the objective, the more formidable must be the actions—unless you're trying to write satire or comedy. To catch a notorious jewel thief, in other words, you'll either send in a master crime stopper like Batman or a bumbling idiot like the Blake Edwards anti-hero Inspector Clouseau, from the *Pink Panther* films.

What extraordinary resistance will the opposition produce in an effort to stop your protagonist, and why?

The obstacles your narrator faces should make readers wonder how they could possibly be overcome. Your villain might appear to be far stronger than your hero (think of Goliath); but ultimately, the narrator proves to be a worthy match in some unexpected or undervalued way (think of David's seemingly primitive slingshot).

What are the consequences of failure for both protagonist and antagonist?

In addition to staging strong conflict in order for your protagonist to achieve a worthy goal, there also ought to be a clear understanding of what will happen if she fails. To give an extreme example, if your protagonist fails to find where a terrorist has planted a bomb, thousands of lives may be lost. If the terrorist fails, then he must commit suicide to fulfill an oath he has taken.

Will this story unfold in a way that keeps me turning the pages, forgetting that I'm reading a book but making me feel I'm experiencing an adventure?

The goal of every writer is to tell his or her story so well that readers will forget about processing words on a page and will vicariously experience the drama instead. This is probably the toughest challenge in creative writing, and it is one that you can meet by plotting your story well, creating realistic characters, and being mindful of style (strong sentences, evocative details, precise word choice).

STRUCTURING A MEMOIR

A memoir can be thought of as a nonfiction novel. You must convey the people, places, and circumstances of your life as accurately as possible. Nonetheless, you are telling a *story* about your life, and any story, fictional or nonfictional, has to have a beginning, middle, and conclusion in which the conflict or crisis is at least partly resolved.

You would think that memoirs are the easiest to write; after all, they're about your experiences, bad and good. In fact, all those experiences of yours are part of the reasons memoirs are tough to write: There's too much to choose from. So the first order of business is to figure out which experiences are most worth writing about (i.e., are most worth sharing with a wide audience). What is it about your experiences that anyone else can learn from? The next step is to figure out how to weave those experiences into a coherent story.

To work out the structure of your memoir, begin with a mental inventory of the events in your life you want to cover. Do not simply begin with "your earliest memories" and proceed in rote chronological sequence from there. Bor-r-r-ing! Instead, your inventory list might include the following:

- My three greatest interests and how they influenced my life
  - Studying ancient languages, especially Latin
  - Biblical archaeology, especially the archaeology of the Temple Mount in Jerusalem
  - Musical instruments, especially percussion instruments
- Things about myself I don't like
  - I am quick tempered
  - I am overly concerned about my appearance
  - I have difficulty socializing
  - I am moody; I get depressed too easily
  - I am too competitive with my siblings
- My most memorable experiences

Once you have filled several pages like this, you can get a better sense of how to organize your memoir.

FOR YOUR WRITER'S NOTEBOOK

1. Prepare scratch outlines based on three or four of the story ideas you have thus far collected.
2. Develop the scratch outlines you've prepared based on two of your story ideas and expand them into a formal outline.
3. Take one of those expanded outlines and prepare a skeletal synopsis of the story.
4. Prepare a scratch outline, a formal outline, and a synopsis for Poe's "Facts in the Case of M. Valdemar."
5. See what you can do with one of the story ideas that follows. First work up a scratch outline for it; next, develop the scratch

outline into a formal outline; finally, write a synopsis based on the formal outline. If you're pleased with the results, begin drafting the story.

    a. Members of a white supremacist group collectively win a major lottery jackpot

    b. Woman rummaging through an old trunk finds evidence that her paternal grandfather robbed a bank and that the loot was never recovered

    c. Man who keeps having visions of the world 50 years in the future discovers that he is from the future

    d. An escaped slave joins the Union Army intending to avenge his former owner

    e. A homeless woman enters a chess tournament

6. Prepare a set of storyboards to sequence the story idea you've developed in exercise 5.

7. Prepare a scratch outline, followed by a formal outline, followed by a skeletal synopsis, and finally an extended synopsis of one possible chapter for your memoir. Here are a few prompts to get you started:

    a. That unforgettable first date (alternative: my flubbed first dates and what went wrong)

    b. The amazing thing I discovered about my father or other family member when I picked the lock on his or her desk drawer

    c. A party I never should have attended

    d. The day I heard my professional (or religious) calling

CHAPTER 7

Working an Idea, Stage IV:

DEVELOPING YOUR IDEAS THROUGH RESEARCH

A little learning is a dangerous thing; Drink deep, or touch not the Pierian spring. —ALEXANDER POPE

I'm a research nerd. Libraries and museums are my amusement parks: Once there, I get caught up in a sleuthing adventure, tracking down material that may have been overlooked or ignored for ages. Just to-day as I write (February 2012), I learned that art historians discovered, via X-ray analysis, that a Mona Lisa "twin" hanging in Madrid's Prado Museum was not painted centuries after the original, as everyone as-sumed, but by one of Leonardo da Vinci's own apprentices working side by side with the Renaissance master while he was painting the original. We now have a different understanding of Leonardo's working habits and teaching methods. Research can change our knowledge of the past in the blink of an eye.

Here is another example: One of the items on display in a special Abraham Lincoln exhibit at the Museum of American History in Washington, D.C., in 2009 (the bicentennial of Lincoln's birth) was the lace cuff of the nurse who assisted the physician attending the president after he'd been shot and subsequently carried across the street from Ford's Theatre to a boardinghouse. The cuff is so easy to disregard—but look a little closer and you see a stain of Lincoln's blood. All of a sudden that terrible event became a palpable experience. I was transfixed. In that bloodstained lace cuff lurked an idea for a story that could further illuminate one of the best known moments in American history—a story, say, dramatizing the manner in which Lincoln was cared for, decades before modern medical practice, between the time he was shot and the time he died, shortly after 7 a.m. the following morning, on April 15, 1865.

RESEARCHING YOUR STORY IDEA

So far, you have invested a lot of time and thought into your story idea, one that you recognized through attentive observation or conjured up in a moment of creative brainstorming and then painstakingly nurtured via free-associating, listing, mapping, and outlining into a story premise. Along the way, perhaps, you jotted down questions about your subject—questions relating to particular events, locations, persons—details you know you ought to include in your work in progress if it is to engage readers and give your narrative the authenticity and accuracy it needs. These prewriting strategies, which I discuss in Chapters 3 and 4, are effective means of rediscovering ideas and experiences already embedded in memory—your tacit knowledge. I like to think of it as conducting research on yourself: your brain as library! Similarly, when you begin researching your story in earnest, you once again conduct a mental inventory of what you already know. It could make your conventional research activities more efficient.

Following your mental inventory of what you already know about your story in progress, you will need to conduct two kinds of research tasks. The first kind I like to call "immersion research," when you learn all you can about your protagonist's livelihood, family situation, physical surroundings. If your story is set in the past, you'll also need to learn about that particular historical milieu.

Next, there's "specific research"—the search for information you must obtain in order to develop a particular scene or convincingly describe a particular action, such as loading and firing a revolver or maneuvering a sailboat or excavating an archaeological site. Let's look more closely at each type of research task.

IMMERSION RESEARCH

Some writers insist on thoroughly researching their story or novel idea before doing anything else. In some situations, that may make sense, especially if your story idea is rooted in real-world history. There are many fine examples to learn from. One of my favorites is Jeffery Deaver: In *Garden of Beasts* (2004), set in Berlin during the 1936 Summer Olympics, Deaver tells the story of American hitman Paul Schumann, hired to assassinate a high-ranking Nazi official. In the following passage, note how Deaver creates dramatic immediacy through vivid sensory—and historically accurate—details:

> The greened bronze of Hitler, standing tall above fallen but noble troops, in November 1923 Square, was impressive but it was located in a neighborhood very different from the others Paul Schumann had seen in Berlin. Papers blew in the dusty wind and there was a sour smell of garbage in the air. Hawkers sold cheap merchandise and fruit, and an artist at a rickety cart would draw your portrait for a few

pfennigs. Aging unlicensed prostitutes and young pimps lounged in doorways. Men missing limbs and rigged with bizarre leather and metal prosthetic braces limped or wheeled up and down the sidewalks, begging. One had a sign pinned to his chest: I gave up my legs for my country. What can you give me?

Are you working on an idea for a private eye mystery? Then I advise you to immerse yourself in the world of private investigation and law enforcement if you're not already familiar with these fields. I'm not saying you need to shadow a PI for a few days (although that certainly would prove advantageous), but you do need to learn all you can about the profession, including reasons people choose this career (rather than other law enforcement careers), the typical assignments PIs take on, and their relationships with clients, police, medical examiners, and lawyers. And don't overlook the seemingly insignificant details, such as the way PIs furnish their offices, how they dress, what they enjoy doing when not tailing bad guys. Reading PI novels is important, but not enough; you want to avoid mimicking other writers' ways of creating private investigation scenarios.

If your novel is set in an actual city (think of Robert Parker's Boston in his Spenser mysteries), then you need to acquire extensive knowledge of the layout of that city—the parks, the landmarks, the transportation system, the popular restaurants, the weather patterns. Ideally, you've spent enough time in this city to capture it realistically in your narrative. Even if you opt for a fictional city—Sue Grafton's Santa Teresa, California, is an example—you nevertheless want to bring it to life as if it were an actual place. It will be doubly challenging if the setting is historical as well as actual. Again, Jeffery Deaver's depiction, in *Garden of Beasts*, of Berlin at the time of the Nazis' rise to power is an ideal example. Few things can throw a reader out of a story faster than getting a geographical detail of his city wrong.

SPECIFIC RESEARCH, FACT-CHECKING

After having spent a substantial chunk of time researching the milieu of your novel and having begun a first draft, you will most likely need to locate information specifically related to a particular scene or situation—information you hadn't anticipated beforehand, even after outlining your story. Much of this research you can probably do on the Internet or using your own reference works; but if you're aiming for authenticity and freshness, you may need to obtain materials not so readily available—government documents, say, or unpublished correspondence or original artifacts archived in museums. Make the most of this specialized research by taking ample notes and seeing these excursions as opportunities for generating additional story ideas—not just for your novel in progress but for future works.

Every story needs to seem realistic within the context of its world; this is as true for a fantasy tale set in some magical realm like Tolkien's Middle-earth as it is for a gritty, grim exposé of the lives of miners in a novel like Emile Zola's *Germinal*. The way to ensure this realism is through factual detail. Are you writing a fantasy involving medieval castles? Then you need to convey to readers what the interior of a castle is like. Are you writing about a mining accident? Better make sure you understand the geological and engineering facts behind mining.

PRIMARY-SOURCE RESEARCH MATERIALS

There's another way to slice the research pie other than immersion/specific, and that is distinguishing between primary and secondary research. Let's say you're writing a historical novel about a prospector who heads to California in 1848 at the beginning of the gold rush. To give readers more than a summative account of this event—that is, to go beyond a history textbook account—you want to focus on the human drama as much as possible. The goal is to get readers to vicariously experience the day-by-day—even the moment-by-moment—idea of the excitement, the danger, the hardship, of prospecting for gold in the wilderness back then. You must do what novelists do: create dramatic immediacy through the use of minute details such as digging to the point of exhaustion, experiencing serious injuries, risking death from cave-ins, and so on. Whether you are creating fictional prospectors or highlighting the lives of actual prospectors, you want the details to be authentic. The best way to convey authenticity is to locate the diaries or notebooks or letters of actual prospectors. In other words, locate and examine *primary* sources.

RESEARCH POINTERS

Taking the time to research your story ideas can pay off handsomely. I advise you to consider the following pointers when conducting research of any kind.

1. Plan your research activities before you begin. Knowing what you're looking for will make your searches more efficient. You'll also enable librarians to offer you better assistance with your searches. If you need to access the holdings of a major research library or special archives, you will most likely need to inform the librarian or archivist of your visit ahead of time.

2. Allow for serendipitous discovery. The most pleasurable research occurs when you *stumble* onto things. Serendipity happens when chance meets preparation. You discover something you would not have recognized as important had you not been so immersed in the subject matter. As the psychologist Jerome Bruner puts it, "Discovery favors the well-prepared mind." Examine books on the shelf next to the book you were looking for—or simply take the time to browse the stacks freely, pulling books from the shelf just to see how they handle their respective subjects. Thousands of ideas are lurking there!

3. Prepare a set of questions you want to answer with your research. Sometimes the very act of framing a question can help sharpen your focus and make your investigations more efficient. Posing questions also has a way of developing additional ideas for your story content.

4. Divide your research tasks into manageable segments. Don't try to research everything at once. Aim for depth more than breadth. The deeper you probe, the more fascinating your findings will be . . . and the more memorable a story you will tell.

5. Be patient; allow for plenty of time. Easier said than done, I know. Like so much else having to do with authorship, patience takes a while to cultivate, but it pays off. When you conduct your investigations in an unhurried manner, your concentration improves and you improve the chances for unexpected discoveries to occur.

6. Take copious notes. I love note taking—almost to a fault. The closet in my study is crammed with collections of notes accumulated from researching my several book projects, as well as notes from my graduate-student days. Most are on 4" × 6" index cards. Notes will serve you in many ways: as supplements to storyboards, as prompts for descriptions of settings, as reminders for character traits, and so on. Caution: It's very easy to overdo note taking; stop once you're confident you have enough information to serve your purpose. See also number 8 below.

7. Look for information that can link particular story events to larger historical or social themes. In her novel *Death Comes for the Archbishop* (1927), for example, Willa Cather links a French bishop's struggle to establish a mission in the New Mexico territory to the larger efforts of missionaries to "tame" the wilderness through religious conversion.

8. Know when to stop researching and start writing. Research can become a pretext for not getting to work on drafting your writing project.

A FEW POINTERS REGARDING INTERNET RESEARCH

When it comes to locating basic information quickly, the Internet is a godsend. A few keystrokes and up comes the information you need. Even so, there are ways to make your Internet research even more efficient. Here are a few suggestions:

- Place web addresses for information resources such as Google, Wikipedia, various online dictionaries, museums, major libraries (including the Library of Congress) on your "Favorites" list in order to access them faster.
- Take advantage of hyperlinks that inevitably appear in the accessed articles—they may lead you to uncover important additional data (see also my discussion of serendipity in research in this chapter).
- Locate the websites or social-network pages of individuals who may be able to provide you with additional information.
- Check out the online archives of notable individuals. It is possible these days to access diaries, letters, and other personal papers that have been digitized and made available to the public.
- Always double-check facts by consulting more than one source. There are many spurious information sources in cyberspace.

BUILDING A HOME REFERENCE LIBRARY

I am an unrepentant bibliophile who believes that books—the kind you put on shelves, not the kind you consign to electronic invisibility inside an e-reader—are the staples and talismans of civilization. If you love to write books, you also ought to own them; to cherish their durability, their material beauty, and their easy accessibility; and build a home library.

Books will serve you in countless ways, but I will mention just one of them: by building a collection of reference works. There is nothing quite like the convenience of grabbing a book off the shelf behind you when you need a quick fact check, especially if you've been writing up a storm and do not want to lose momentum by having to visit the library or even exit your file to surf the Internet. This means investing in reference books, most of which are inexpensive, especially when purchased used.

Reference books are also useful for generating ideas, as I discussed in Chapter 2. I mention this here to remind you that you can generate new ideas for stories while in the process of conducting minor research tasks for a present project. For example, if you're writing a story in which eyesight plays a role, you may find yourself checking the definition of technical terms like *scotoma*. When you look up the word, all of a sudden you get an idea for another story:

---

sco•to•ma: [skoh-**toh**-m*uh*] *n.* an area of diminished vision within the visual field. **Story idea:** *Woman is haunted by strange images in her peripheral vision.*
[*American Heritage Dictionary*]

Your essential references shelf ought to consist of the following works:

- **A DESK DICTIONARY, RECENT EDITION.** If you write historical fiction, then I suggest the *Oxford English Dictionary* as well. One- and two-volume microprint editions of the original twenty-volume edition, as well as an abridged "compact" edition, are available. The OED includes the usage history, with examples, of every word in the language.
- **A BIBLE.** I recommend the King James translation, as this is the version most often referenced in literary works. The Bible has had a profound influence upon Western culture for many centuries.

- **A CONCORDANCE TO THE BIBLE.** A concordance tells you how and where every word in the Bible is used. Is the word "sue" used in Scripture? According to *Young's Analytical Concordance to the Bible* (containing 771,000 quotations and references), it is used once, in Matthew 5:40.
- **AN ALMANAC FOR THE CURRENT YEAR.** This one-volume reference is invaluable for its numerous lists (of entertainers past and present, awards, scientific achievements), profiles of every nation on earth, statistics on the economy, athletic events, and census results.
- **AN ENCYCLOPEDIA OF LITERARY WORKS.** See my discussion of *Benet's Reader's Encyclopedia* in the context of writing a synopsis in Chapter 6.
- **A DICTIONARY OF MYTHOLOGY.** Inexpensive one-volume paperback editions are common. Like the narratives and adages of the Bible, the stories of the ancient gods and demigods have been firing up the imaginations of writers for millennia.
- **A DICTIONARY OF QUOTATIONS.** Pithy adages are ideal for generating story ideas as well as for effectively capturing key insights into points you or your characters wish to convey.

FIELD RESEARCH

Scientists, especially geologists, archaeologists, anthropologists, ethnographers, and biologists, aren't the only ones who do research out of doors to examine phenomena or observe activities firsthand. So do novelists. If you're writing a novel about the Revolutionary War, it pays to visit historical sites such as the house in Concord, Massachusetts, where the Minutemen assembled, or General Washington's encampment at Valley Forge, Pennsylvania. In a novel, you want to give readers the feeling of being there through dramatic immediacy. This is easier to accomplish if you visit these places yourself, if feasible. Of course, you can wing it by studying the firsthand accounts of others, but you would almost certainly notice different things. For example, before I visited the ruins of Pompeii, I'd read numerous descriptions (historical and fictional) of before, during, and after Vesuvius erupted in A.D. 79 and buried the town for nearly two millennia. But when I was there, I noticed things I never read about: the eerie shape of the volcanic mountain in the distance; the ruts in the street stones created by many decades of wagon wheels; what it felt like to sit inside a still-intact Pompeiian house and view its wall frescoes. I also hadn't read about the interiors of the town brothels; as you walk through them, you will find yourself surrounded by provocative frescoes—usually depicting an overeager Priapus, ready for action.

No matter how many books you read or how many travel videos you watch about a place you intend to use as the setting for a story, they cannot entirely replace firsthand experience.

INTERVIEWS WITH EXPERTS

If you want to obtain in-depth or "insider" information on a topic, you should plan to interview experts. I'm not referring just to experts in academic subjects, but also to mechanics, construction workers, law enforcement personnel, health care workers, florists, vintners, electricians, computer technicians, locksmiths—anyone who has worked in these fields for some time generally qualifies as an expert.

Here's how to go about setting up and conducting an interview:

1. Contact the individual by phone or e-mail. Describe your project and why you want to interview him or her. Estimate the length of the interview. Be flexible on dates and times.
2. Prepare a list of questions you want the expert to answer. Be prepared to ask "spin-off" questions—i.e., unanticipated questions that are triggered by the expert's answer.
3. Ask for permission to take notes or to record the interview.
4. Ask the expert for permission to contact him or her after the interview for possible follow-up questions.

5. Ask the expert where you might obtain additional inside information on the subject.

In case the individuals you wish to interview are too busy to see you in person, ask for an e-mail or telephone interview.

FOR YOUR WRITER'S NOTEBOOK

1. Prepare a list of "immersion" research tasks for your current work in progress. For each of these tasks, prepare detailed notes and store them in your notebook or card file.

2. Do library or Internet research on a historical site near your home and take notes. Then visit the site when you get a chance, again taking notes. When you return, describe what you learned during the visit that you did not learn through secondary research.

3. Spend a half hour paging randomly through your dictionary and learning the meanings of unfamiliar words. Record these new words and their definitions in your notebook. Next, put down two or three ideas that the new words suggested to you.

4. Here is an exercise in research serendipity: Pull a book off the shelf totally at random—don't even look at the title—and find something in that book that you can relate, either directly or indirectly, to some aspect of the subject of your current writing project.

5. Make an appointment to interview an expert in a subject relevant to your work in progress. Use your writer's notebook to draft a list of questions. After the interview, record the information in your notebook.

6. Imagine that you want to develop a story in the context of one of the following issues. Locate three different informa-

tion sources on the web and summarize the difference in their respective coverage of the topic in question:
- Global warming (or climate change)
- Immigration reform
- Sweatshops
- Media censorship
- Ancient astronauts (as having inspired the pyramid builders, or built the pyramids themselves?)

7. Visit a research library, museum, or art gallery in your community and locate information about one of the artifacts or works of art on display. Record the highlights of your investigation in your notebook. Later, generate a story idea based on this research.

8. Imagine that you are planning to write a narrative on the boyhood years of one of our presidents. Locate appropriate library and Internet resources. Here are a few suggestions:
- The website of the presidential library for this president
- Biographies (there will be many; compare each biographer's treatment of the subject)
- Historical novels in which this future president is a character; try to determine which incidents are authentic, which the novelist invented
- Articles (print and Internet); use Google to locate bibliographies as well as articles published online

CHAPTER 8

Working With Ideas, Stage V:

TAKING THE LEAP OF FAITH: WRITING A FIRST DRAFT

I write the big scenes first, the scenes that carry the meaning of the book.

—JOYCE CARY

No matter how meticulously you plan (and if you've been following all the advice in this book, you have indeed been planning meticulously), the actual writing of a first draft can be scary. All of the prewriting activities—the brainstorming, freewriting, mapping, outlining, and sculpting—have been for your eyes only. Even the freewriting, which superficially resembles drafting, is private because it's designed to dredge stuff out of your subconscious and up to the surface, so that you can see your own thoughts and learn to bypass the overzealous editor in your skull. A draft, even a first draft, is for readers' eyes. Not that you're obliged to actually give it to somebody to read, mind you, but you should write a first draft as if you plan to do just that.

But here's where the leap of faith comes in: Human beings have a marvelous ability to tell a story spontaneously once the basic story idea is in place. That's because every sentence you write (or speak aloud) becomes a setup for the next sentence and the next one after that.

Unlike preparing an outline or even a synopsis of your story, writing a first draft means actually bringing a story world into being. Moreover, you are not just the creator, but part of the creation in the sense that unanticipated events, settings, and character interaction will pop out of nowhere once you set your story into motion.

MOMENTUM

Writers sometimes talk about gaining momentum while drafting. They reach a point in the draft where the story seems to unfold by itself, and the characters take on lives of their own. Meanwhile the writer, as James Joyce once put it, sits back and pares his fingernails. To make this happen, internalize the basic story you want to tell; profile your characters ahead of time in such detail that they feel as if you've known them a long time. On the other hand, avoid obsessing over such minutiae as what your characters should do with their hands while they're conversing or whether to let readers know if they've shut the door behind them or which pant leg they step into first when dressing. To put it another way, you want to give your characters enough flexibility for them to say and do things on their own, arising from the dynamics of any given moment that you've set into motion. It's really not as mysterious as it sounds. Just as in real life we cannot anticipate what comes out of our mouths in conversation, so, too, in fiction, people will do things that could not have been anticipated ahead of time—yet nonetheless the things they do seem inevitable.

DRAFTING DYNAMICS

Movie scenes are not filmed in the sequence presented in the script but rather according to setting. Thus scenes with similar interior settings may be filmed separately from those with external settings. Similarly, when you are working on the draft of a novel, a memoir, or even a short story, you would do well to draft first those segments of the narrative you feel best prepared to complete. For example, many novelists will draft the conclusion before anything else because they want to make sure everything else moves coherently toward that ending. J.K. Rowling is known to have written the last sentence of her last book very early on.

If you're writing a novel in which you shift viewpoint from one principal character to another in alternating chapters (a common technique), you may want to draft all the Viewpoint Character A chapters before drafting the Viewpoint Character B or C chapters (one more reason why outlines are so useful).

Let me suggest yet another way to write a first draft: speed drafting. It is similar to freewriting (see Chapter 2), except that you're now writing with a basic plan in mind, and you have an outline to consult. Speed drafting borders on the reckless, so let's weigh the advantages and the disadvantages. The advantages are these:

- You're experiencing the story almost as if you were reading it, thereby giving you a better feel for its progression, its rhythms.
- You will finish the draft of a book in about two or three months (assuming you write four or five pages a day).
- Writing quickly means you're less likely to generate verbose, ponderous prose; you're concentrating on story rather than style.
- You're less tempted to revise on the spot, thereby maintaining momentum.
- As with freewriting, speed drafting may generate intrastory ideas more readily (because you're in free-association mode).

Now consider the disadvantages:

- You feel tempted to simplify your story, to cut corners, to eschew nuance, to make compromising choices that will be difficult to undo later on.
- Rushing through anything is seldom a pleasant experience; it could raise your blood pressure. Speed drafting turns what should be a pleasurable experience into drudgery.
- You're less likely to experience the story as a reader might.

At least in terms of quantity, advantages outweigh the disadvantages, so I recommend that you give speed drafting a try.

One last suggestion for what you can do if you wish to complete the draft of a novel quickly: participate in National Novel Writing Month (every November).

A FEW SUGGESTIONS FOR DRAFTING PAINLESSLY, PRODUCTIVELY, EVEN PLEASURABLY

Even the best-prepared writers—those who have a clear sense of the story's overall design, who have outlined the plot dutifully and profiled their characters in detail—sometimes have a tough time getting the day's writing going. Why is that?

I can think of several reasons, having been guilty of all of them at one time or another. Here is the commonest reason: uncertainty. You balk at the thought of committing the story to paper; you worry that your writing won't pass muster; maybe you should do more research, more planning first; you wonder if you're wasting your time. Another reason is insufficient energy. After all, you have a day job! You've got a family who needs your presence!

Are you beset by such anxieties? Then here's what you need to tell yourself:

SHUT UP AND WRITE

There are plenty of excuses you can come up with to keep from hitting that keyboard and producing a manuscript. Not only should you stop fretting, you should learn to enjoy the sensation of creating a story, of writing a book. But enough pep talk. I promised you suggestions for a painless start, so here they are:

1. **DO A QUICK REREADING OF YOUR OUTLINE.** This is to refresh your memory of the story elements and the plot structure. The better you've internalized the story, the less likely you'll overlook important plot points while drafting.

2. **USE YOUR OUTLINE AS A TEMPLATE.** Just paste it into your draft file and fill in the blanks (reformatting, of course). Now you can invent additional story content without having to keep checking back on your outline.

3. **THINK "TELLING YOUR STORY" RATHER THAN "WRITING THE FIRST DRAFT."** Better yet, think of telling your story to an eager, waiting audience.

4. **CREATE VISUAL AIDS (DRAWINGS, COLLAGES, AND SUCH) OF SCENES FROM YOUR STORY AND WORK PART OF THE NARRATIVE AROUND THEM.** (See also Chapter 2.) The illustrations will help you develop the particulars of a scene. Who knows, you might decide to include them with the final draft of your manuscript, especially if you're writing for children or young adults.

5. **IF THE EDITOR IN YOUR HEAD STARTS KICKING AND SCREAMING, INSISTING YOU REVISE EVERY PARAGRAPH BEFORE PROCEEDING TO THE NEXT, GAG HIM.** You can set him free as soon as the draft is completed.

6. **SKIP AROUND.** As I mentioned earlier, it isn't necessary to tell your story in sequence. If you run out of steam while developing one scene or narrative line, shift over to another one. This technique can help reinforce your memory of what happens in earlier stages of the story.

7. **WRITE THE BIG SCENES FIRST.** These are the major confrontation or revelation scenes, the moments in your story that smaller scenes move toward. Getting the big scenes drafted first will make the smaller scenes easier to write.

8. **USE YOUR STORYBOARDS TO HELP FLESH OUT THE SCENES.** Storyboarding allows you to better visualize the many scenes in your novel or memoir; it also helps you with sequencing those scenes. (See Chapter 6.)

9. **CONSIDER DICTATING YOUR DRAFT INTO A TAPE RECORDER.** Some writers, yours truly among them, freeze up when it comes to drafting anything orally. But if this method works for you, your drafting speed could increase dramatically. Caution: Speak slowly unless you type extremely fast—or you have an assistant who can.

10. **DON'T WORRY ABOUT YOUR DAILY QUOTA WHILE YOU'RE DRAFTING.** A quota should be one that you aim for but not necessarily one that you must attain at all costs—too much anxiety gets generated that way, and anxiety is bad for creativity.

11. **STOP IN THE MIDDLE OF A SENTENCE.** This was one of Ernest Hemingway's little tricks to help him get back into drafting mode the next day; presumably, it will help you throttle up more quickly. Never stop at the end of a chapter or section, though; it's too hard to get going again!

12. **RELISH THE EXPERIENCE OF BRINGING SOMETHING NEW INTO THE WORLD.** Here is where the pleasure of drafting comes in. As you write, remind yourself now and then of the magic of telling a story that no one has ever heard before. There is much satisfaction to be reaped from this experience but the hard work all too often obscures it.

THE LEAP OF FAITH

The ever-quotable Ralph Waldo Emerson tells us in his essay "Self-Reliance" to "Trust thyself: every heart vibrates to that iron string."

Have faith in the fact that you can complete a book-length draft; and even if it doesn't turn out quite the way you want it to (as is the case with most first drafts even by professional novelists), you will be able to bring it up to snuff later on. Oh, and here is another bit of Emersonian wisdom from that same essay: "In every work of genius we recognize our own rejected thoughts." Dwell on that for a moment: Being part of a society that tends to overvalue the status quo, we get a little queasy when it comes to sharing our original thoughts, especially if they're controversial or risqué or just plain weird in the eyes of most people. Yet, ironically, the best of those controversial, risqué, or weird ideas become the talk of the town. Consider these examples:

- Harry G. Frankfurt, a Princeton philosophy professor, dares to follow through with his idea on writing a book about bullshit (*On Bullshit*) and it becomes a bestseller.
- The late French novelist, Georges Perec, writes a 285-page parody of a political thriller, *A Void*, without ever using the letter e, the most frequently used letter in the alphabet (talk about getting an idea out of the blue!); just as remarkably, Perec's English translator, Gilbert Adair, manages never to use the letter e as well.
- Spencer Quinn has been writing a series of mystery novels told from the point of view of the detective's dog: *Dog on It*; *Thereby Hangs a Tail*; *To Fetch a Thief*; etc.
- In *The Handmaid's Tale*, Canadian novelist Margaret Atwood tells the story of a postapocalyptic world in which radiation has rendered most women sterile, and in which the very few fertile women are recruited as "handmaids."
- In *Myra Breckinridge*, Gore Vidal's heroine is a transsexual dominatrix who upends Hollywood-reinforced stereotypes of gender and sexuality.

Literature is filled with examples like these. Imagine if those novelists decided their ideas were too offbeat to push ahead with a first draft.

MEETING SPECIFIC
DRAFTING OBJECTIVES

There is much to keep in mind about your story during the drafting stage. Telling a story means telling what the different characters—protagonist, antagonist, supporting characters, background characters—are doing and saying. This in turn means keeping track of the distinctive personalities, speech mannerisms, eccentricities, and so on. Then there are the settings, interior and exterior, that must be conveyed with just the right verbal brushstrokes at the proper time. All the while you need to ensure that the suspense or intrigue is mounting, and that the confrontations are powerful and genuine. Drafting is multitasking to be sure.

If you've done enough groundwork—the character profiling, the outlining, the storyboarding—you should have no serious problems orchestrating the story elements. But even with the advance preparation, it's easy to lose track of things. Besides spreading out your notes and tacking storyboard cards to your corkboards, you might also try preparing the following checklist of the specific tasks that need to be accomplished in each chapter. Keep this list in view as you work on the draft:

CHAPTER OBJECTIVES PROMPT SHEET

CHAPTER _____

TARGET DATE FOR COMPLETION _____

What is taking place in this chapter_____

_____

_____

_____

The principal actors in this chapter and what each intends to do and/or tries to do and/or actually accomplishes or fails to accomplish _____

_____

_____

Ideas, themes, conveyed either directly or indirectly in this chapter_____

_____

_____

The setting(s) for this chapter (interior, exterior) _____

_____

_____

Plot progression: advance(s), setback(s), new complication(s) in this chapter

_____

_____

Teaser ending/transition to next chapter _____

_____

_____

No matter how well you establish drafting objectives, however, unanticipated ideas and techniques will occur to you—and that's important. Creativity thrives on the unanticipated. A story too carefully planned runs the risk of sounding too methodical. Readers crave freshness to storytelling, and that is what spontaneous inventiveness delivers.

FOR YOUR WRITER'S NOTEBOOK

1. Maintain a log of your drafting progress, at least for the first week. Your log should consist of the following information:

- The time you began drafting
- The amount of time you spent writing before taking a break
- The number of words and/or pages you wrote (including partial pages) before taking a break
- A summary of the day's drafting
- An overview of what you intend to work on tomorrow

2. Prepare a Chapter Objectives Prompt Sheet for each day's drafting.

3. If you find yourself unable to begin or resume working on your draft, respond to the following questions in your notebook:

   a. What is keeping you from working on your draft?

   b. What do you need to do to overcome that obstacle?

   c. Have you made the effort to overcome the obstacle? Why or why not?

4. Instead of aiming for a first draft, do a quick discovery draft, which is a kind of focused freewriting. You might wind up with a lot of chaff, but at least you will have made it into draft mode.

5. Draft a key scene from your novel, even if you haven't finished working out the plot in its entirety.

6. Prepare a tentative chapter-by-chapter synopsis.

7. Draft the first chapter. If you don't feel ready to tackle an entire chapter, then draft the opening scene from that first chapter.

8. Once you have drafted the first chapter, return to your chapter-by-chapter synopsis and revise it based on new ideas generated from having written the first chapter. Continue this strategy with each subsequent chapter you draft.

CHAPTER 9

Working an Idea, Stage VI:

My pencils outlast their erasers.

—VLADIMIR NABOKOV

To revise means literally to re-see, to re-envision the story you've been struggling to develop from your basic idea for the past several months. Although we've been considering the various tasks associated with working an idea from inception to draft as "stages" (implying a linear progression), these stages are often interchangeable and recursive. For example, you may begin working an idea by plunging immediately into a draft and letting the idea evolve through trial and error. Then you may pause to do some brainstorming and/or mapping and restart by revising the portion of the draft you've produced. The problem with this method, of course, is enduring several false starts; however, it is well suited to those writers with more impulsive temperaments, who find it difficult to plan ahead.

I myself tend to revise as I go along, but I'm not a fanatic about it. What I often do is insert a double-bracketed reminder, such as [[*Go into more detail about this*]], following a problematic passage so that I'll be less inclined to disrupt my drafting momentum.

I think the main reason I'm always tempted to revise, even before completing page one of a first draft, is that I *enjoy* revising. Some writers hate revising; they get annoyed with themselves for "not getting it right the first time." For them, writing is a chore at best, and the faster the job is done, the better. I wonder if the schoolmarm obsession with correctness is the culprit here. I was subjected to that sort of thing myself, as I explained in my discussion of outlining in Chapter 6, and it took me a long time to deprogram myself—or I should say partially deprogram myself, as I keep wanting to revise virtually every sentence I write before moving on to the next. What prevents me from doing so is my promise to myself that I will allot plenty of time for revision provided I work productively on my first draft.

TWO KINDS OF REVISING

There are two kinds of revising: surface and substantive. Surface revising consists of copyediting, the purpose of which is to improve the prose style—that is, to make the writing more readable. Here are several typical examples of copyediting tasks:

REPLACE WEAK VERBS WITH STRONG ONES. For example, instead of "Janice *has* a beautiful singing voice," write "Janice *sings* beautifully" (which also results in a more concise, hence more readable, sentence).

CHANGE PASSIVE VOICE TO ACTIVE VOICE TO CLARIFY WHO IS DOING WHAT. For example, revise "War was declared" to

"Sarvonia declared war on Alporia." (Sometimes it really pays to know who does what to whom!)

TRANSFORM A WORDY SENTENCE INTO A CONCISE ONE.
Wordiness interferes with ease of reading and makes the content more difficult to understand. Learning to write concisely takes time to master; you need to train your eye to spot verbosity. Here are a few pointers:

- Look for sluggish phrases, especially *there* + a form of the verb *to be*, and sluggish noun phrases. Stripping a sentence of such excess verbiage renders the sentence a lot more readable. Example:

  > **WORDY:** There is a tendency among first-year college students to avoid taking prerequisite courses in writing.
  > **MORE CONCISE:** First-year students tend to avoid writing courses. ("There is" deleted; noun phrase "a tendency" turned into a strong verb.)

- Look for opportunities to embed separate bits of information in as many short sentences into a single sentence. Example:

  > **WORDY:** Louis has a pet cat. His name is Shadow. Shadow likes to eat mackerel.
  > **MORE CONCISE:** Louis's cat, Shadow, likes to eat mackerel. Or even more concisely: Louis's cat, Shadow, likes mackerel. (What else would the cat do with it?)

- Remove unnecessary adjectives and adverbs; let nouns and verbs do most of the work in conveying meaning. Example:

  > **REDUNDANT USE OF ADJECTIVES:** Tom was extremely outraged by his angry brother's very insensitive remarks.
  > **REVISION:** Tom was outraged by his brother's insensitive remarks.

Less is more! The statement is more forceful without the inten-
sifiers *extremely* and *very*; no meaning is lost because *outraged*
implies extreme emotion.

- Avoid inappropriate use of jargon. Jargon is specialized language,
and every profession has its own kind of jargon. In biochemistry,
for example, terms like "chlorinated hydrocarbons" and "sys-
temic insecticides" would confuse the general reader unless they
were defined in passing. Note how Rachel Carson introduces the
latter concept to a lay audience in her classic work, *Silent Spring*:

> The world of systemic insecticides is a weird world, sur-
> passing the imaginings of the brothers Grimm—perhaps
> most closely akin to the cartoon world of Charles Ad-
> dams. . . . It is a world where a flea bites a dog, and dies be-
> cause the dog's blood has been made poisonous. . . . What
> makes an insecticide a systemic is the ability to permeate
> all the tissues of a plant or animal and make them toxic.

(By the way, Carson's book is a marvelous example of the
way in which expressive language—the language of storytelling and poetry—can help readers comprehend complex
scientific ideas.)

**IMPROVE READABILITY BY VARYING SENTENCE LENGTH
AND EMPHASIS.** Instead of a string of short, choppy sentences, try
to vary sentence length. Such variation will make your narrative voice
more distinctive. Strings of sentences with the same construction tend
to make you sound like a robot. For example:

> **STRING OF MONOTONE SENTENCES:** Dorothy
> awoke. The sun was shining through the trees. Toto
> had long been out chasing birds and squirrels. She sat
> up and looked around her. She noticed the scarecrow.
> He was still standing patiently in his corner. He was
> waiting for her.

> **REVISED FOR SENTENCE VARIETY:** When Dorothy awoke the sun was shining through the trees and Toto had long been out chasing birds and squirrels. She sat up and looked around her. There was the Scarecrow, still standing patiently in his corner, waiting for her.
>
> (L. Frank Baum, *The Wonderful Wizard of Oz*)

Caution: The above examples of copyediting are out of context, so it's conceivable that each of them is just fine as originally written in certain contexts. Exceptions to even the most sensible guidelines always exist, but you should at least be aware of the guidelines before overriding them. For example, that rule about using active voice rather than passive voice: It makes sense when you're in narrative mode ("The dog was walked" just doesn't work); but if you're preparing a lab report, it's not necessary to show agency—"Phosphoric acid was added to the solution" is perfectly appropriate.

The second kind of surface revision is *proofreading*, where you correct errors in spelling, grammar, mechanics, punctuation, and formatting, and you check for typos or omitted passages or incorrect dates, facts, and figures.

Copyediting and proofreading are late-stage revision tasks, formally undertaken after a final draft has been completed and your manuscript is being readied for publication. Before this "polishing" can take place, you have to come up with a final draft, one in which your story is fully developed in terms of plot, character, theme, and authenticity. Ensuring these criteria is the aim of substantive revision, which could take as long to finish as the first draft.

If superficial revising means going through your draft with a fine-tooth comb, substantive revising means going through your draft with a machete. With substantive revising you show no mercy: You hack away chunks of static plot, unconvincing character behavior, insufficiently delineated confrontation scenes, weak description of setting or situation, chunks of flat summary where there should be dramatic immediacy, suspense, and wonder over what is going to happen next. Such revising can mean the difference between a publishable manuscript or not. Sometimes a first draft simply has to be tossed, in which case you take a deep breath and, as F. Scott Fitzgerald famously put it, you revise "from spirit."

STRATEGIES FOR SUBSTANTIVE REVISION

Substantive revision requires a lot of hard, patient work. However, it really isn't as painful as it may seem at first. After all, you're not discarding the basic story line or the characters or the settings but rather simply investing them with new energy and insight. Okay, you have to start from scratch because your story idea was problematic to begin with. It might not have been fresh enough, logical enough, captivating enough; but you inevitably learn from such false starts, so they are never a waste of time.

Writing well, as you've undoubtedly discovered by now, demands a lot of patient, disciplined work for which you must recruit in equal measure the logic centers and the imagination centers of your brain. It requires a lot of patience and persistence as well, because forging ideas into stories involves a lot of hit and miss—that is, a lot of planning and drafting and replanning and revising.

Unlike speaking informally or dashing off e-mails to friends, creating a work of fiction or a memoir involves considerable multitasking: developing an engaging narrative, going into sufficient detail, creating suspense and mood, providing enough backstory, and so on. Is it any wonder things don't come out right the first time, or the second time?

For many writers (including yours truly) the toughest part of writing is getting that first draft finished. Even with your outline, synopsis, character profiles, storyboarded scene sequences, and research notes spread out before you, plunging into a first draft is akin to plunging into cold water. My advice: Bite the bullet and *plunge*; don't agonize over every word or sentence. There's a good reason I say this: Having a completed first draft gives you a much better opportunity to fine-tune your story than trying to fine-tune your story while the draft is in progress.

THE RELATIONSHIP BETWEEN IDEA AND VOICE

If you want your story idea to flourish, you need to cultivate your literary voice to ensure that it will convey your story as clearly, as forcefully, and as engagingly as possible. Just as each of us has a distinctive speaking voice, so do we have a potentially distinctive writing voice. I say "potentially" because bad or undeveloped writing habits will muffle that voice, just as holding a hand over your mouth will muffle your ability to speak clearly.

The late John Updike—distinguished novelist, short story writer, and a masterful stylist—elegantly conveyed the importance of style in his National Book Award acceptance speech (for *The Centaur*) in March 1964: "Anyone dignified with the name of 'writer' should strive, surely, to discover or invent the verbal texture that most closely corresponds to the tone of life as it arrives on his nerves. . . . Is the sentence plastic enough to render the flux, the blurring, the endless innuendo of experience as we feel it?"[2]

One of the most important goals in substantive revision, then, is to ensure that you are saying precisely what you want to say, in your most authentic voice. Readers look for *personality* in the prose, and that is why you must take care to make your prose reflect the way you really sound. The worst thing you can do is to try to sound "objective"—save that for your business reports.

Now then, cultivating one's voice is not as simple as it sounds. If I tell you "to sound like yourself," I am assuming that your natural voice is one that readers would find engaging. But that begs the question: "What should my natural voice ideally be like?" After all, some people's natural voices seem flat, uninspired, and unnuanced instead of distinctive, engaging, and authoritative. To put it another way, how natural is natural? Are there ways to make one's natural voice more distinctive, more engaging, more authoritative? Two things are important here, and each depends upon the other to succeed:

- Being attuned to the conversation of humanity
- Being well read

BEING ATTUNED TO THE CONVERSATION OF HUMANITY

Writers, typically, are keenly aware of human events, globally and locally. They are activists, only they act through written discourse more than through physical involvement. Only rarely do they cut themselves off from society to sequester themselves in a garret or ivory tower, as the stereotypes would have you believe. This social activism requires a distinctive voice—but distinctiveness is a relative term, resting on the bedrock of convention, just as the most innovative works of literature rely to some extent on standards of grammar and usage. My point here is that substantive revision will help you to cultivate that voice only if you're familiar with the kaleidoscopic voices that make up the conversation of humankind. To write for publication regardless of genre is to be engaged in the conversation of humanity.

BEING WELL READ

The voice you are trying to cultivate in your writing is greatly influenced by your reading. Writers in all fields share a foundation of canonical readings—what used to be referred to as "the great books" even though this canon has changed over the past forty years as a result of heightened multicultural awareness. In addition to the classics of Western literature, which include the works of Homer, Dante, Shakespeare, Cervantes, Wordsworth, Keats, the Brontë sis-

ters, Dickens, Emerson, Thoreau, Hawthorne, Whitman, and Dickinson, masterpieces by Asian and African writers, and hitherto underrepresented ethnic groups in the United States, are now included. As a writer wishing to contribute his or her voice to today's conversation of humankind, it is to your advantage to be well read in this new global canon.

LEVELS OF FORMALITY

There is another way to think about the elusive subject of voice, and that is by distinguishing among the different levels of formality. Let's start with speech. At informal gatherings among friends and relatives, we would most likely speak colloquially, informally, casually, without much attention to verbal or even grammatical precision. But if we find ourselves the next day speaking to a judge in court or giving a speech, we will use formal diction and syntax.

Similarly, there are levels of formality in writing, not counting the writing that tries to capture the different levels of speech formality mentioned above. Authors can narrate their stories through different levels of formality, depending on the nature of the narrator. In narrating through his preadolescent protagonists, Mark Twain chose a colloquial backwoods style appropriate to those characters. You probably recall those unforgettable opening lines from *Adventures of Huckleberry Finn*:

> You don't know about me, without you have read a book
> by the name of "The Adventures of Tom Sawyer," but
> that ain't no matter. That book was made by Mr. Mark
> Twain, and he told the truth, mainly. There was things
> which he stretched, but mainly he told the truth. . . I
> never seen anybody but lied one time or another, without it was Aunt Polly, or the widow, or maybe Mary.

Between the casual, informal voice and the formal voice are several other kinds of voices:

- **JARGON OR IN-GROUP SPEECH:** Jargon of professionals (see the Rachel Carson passage, page 118) and jargon of subcultures such as prison jargon and mob jargon.
- **SATIRE, HUMOR:** This kind of voice makes frequent use of hyperbole (exaggeration), as in this passage by Woody Allen, who in "A Look at Organized Crime" ridicules Mob subculture by exaggerating the way they use character descriptors for their middle names.

> In 1921, Thomas (The Butcher) Covello and Ciro (The Tailor) Santucci attempted to organize disparate ethnic groups of the underworld and thus take over Chicago. This was foiled when Albert (The Logical Positivist) Corillo assassinated Kid Lipsky.

GETTING FEEDBACK ON YOUR FIRST DRAFT

Here is how I distinguish a rough draft or discovery draft from a first draft: A discovery draft is for your eyes only. It represents writing in order to discover what it is you want to say, which later may or may not serve as a prompt for shaping a later draft. A first draft, by contrast, represents writing that is good enough to show to someone for feedback. You can be your own worst critic (and you need to be), but that does not guarantee you will catch all the problems.

Remember what I said about the importance of audience awareness. Writing means writing to be read, writing for a wide audience. Knowing that people will be reading your words serves as a constant reminder not to get careless or lazy.

The best feedback you can get is from an experienced reader, ideally someone whose relationship with you does not result in a conflict of interest. A spouse or close friend will work provided he or she can be uncompromisingly objective and is not worried about hurting

your feelings. Assure such a reader, nonetheless, that you have a thick skin and want only the bluntest criticism.

Participating in writers' groups or workshops can be extremely helpful. Typically, you receive feedback from several other writers, which together can provide you with an ample slate of revision strategies. A note of caution, though: Sometimes such feedback misses the point of what you were trying to do. If that is the case, ignore them; however, make doubly sure there isn't something you can rework that would prevent such misreading.

To give or receive useful feedback, I recommend that you use (or have others use) a first draft critique sheet—one similar to the following:

FIRST DRAFT CRITIQUE SHEET

Working title: _____

Name of reader: _____

Overall strengths of the draft:_____
_____
_____
_____

Basic problem(s) with the draft:_____
_____
_____
_____

[Specific suggestions for improvement]

Opening segment (snags interest? conflict situation clearly established?)
_____
_____

Characters (fully delineated? behavioral and physical characteristics described in sufficient detail?)

_____

_____

_____

Setting, internal and external (realistically and vividly depicted?)

_____

_____

_____

Goal (urgent? vital? challenging?)

_____

_____

_____

Conflict situation (sufficiently developed? reader interest sustained?)

_____

_____

_____

Concluding segment (conflict satisfyingly resolved? loose ends tied?)

_____

_____

_____

Mood, tone (lighthearted? serious? satirical? consistent tone throughout?)

_____

_____

Theme ("so what" question answered?)

_____

_____

Style (sentence structure, word choice, paragraphing)

_____

_____

_____

Other comments:

_____

_____

_____

A WORD ABOUT WORKSHOPS

Writers' workshops also give you the opportunity to read and give feedback on the manuscripts of others. This experience will sharpen your ability to critique your own work as well as introduce you to different methods of storytelling.

Many kinds of writing workshops exist, from relatively informal gatherings in a host writer's home to weekend or weeklong writers' retreats (often featuring well-known guest writers) to two- or three-year M.F.A. programs. There are also online writing courses available, such as those sponsored by Writer's Digest University. You can sign up for a course in the basics of effective writing, in plotting, in advanced novel writing. Check out the options at www.writersonlineworkshops.com.

You can find weekend or weeklong conferences for writers anywhere in the country. Most are held during the summer. Here is a small sampling:

- North Carolina Writers' Network
- StoryStudio Chicago
- Santa Barbara (CA) Writers Conference
- Napa Valley Writers' Conference
- Jackson Hole (WY) Writers Conference
- Writing the Rockies

- ThrillerFest (held once a year [in July] in midtown Manhattan)
- Wesleyan Writers Conference (Wesleyan University)

Information about these and other writing conferences, retreats, and courses can be accessed online.

FOR YOUR WRITER'S NOTEBOOK

1. Use your writer's notebook now and then to practice concision. For starters, revise the following sentences to make them more concise:

   a. It has come to our attention that our company's profits have exhibited a reduction of 10 percent during the course of the last few years.

   b. Gary's acceptance of Mary's gift was done with gratitude.

   c. Pauline had come up with a plan for doing a thorough analysis of her investment portfolio.

2. Revise the sentences in the following passage to improve readability:

   Sharon did not want to enter the abandoned house. She did not believe in ghosts. However, she frightened easily. Her friend Karen made fun of her. "It's just an old empty house," Karen said. Sharon would not relent. Karen then said she would tell everyone how Sharon was afraid of her own shadow.

3. Dig out the draft of a story you wrote a while back and revise it based on the following criteria:

   - Depth of characterization
   - Clarity and significance of protagonist's goal
   - Strength and believability of the opposition
   - Effectiveness of the opening

- Pacing, tension, buildup toward climax or revelation
- Mood, atmosphere
- Effectiveness of the climax or revelation
- Effectiveness of the conclusion

4. Another antidote to writer's block is to read works outside your usual area of interest. As you read, take notes on the following:
   a. Facts you didn't know before
   b. Information you might use to help you with a work in progress or the revision of a completed work
   c. Ideas you get from the work that you could transform into stories or narrative essays

5. Exchange first drafts of a story with a fellow writer and critique each other's work using the first draft critique sheet presented above. After filling out the sheet, share your comments orally with the author. That way, you'll have a chance to elaborate on your comments and the author will have an opportunity to ask follow-up questions.

6. Before revising a draft, read it aloud to a friend (or to yourself, or to your pet cat if you don't mind feeling a bit silly). Reason: When reading aloud you will be able to catch clumsy sentences or problems with coherence.

PART 2

Applications

Time flies.

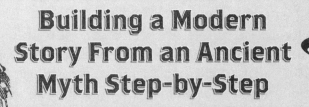

CHAPTER 10

Building a Modern Story From an Ancient Myth Step-by-Step

Writers have been mining ideas for stories, poems, and plays from ancient stories ever since, well, ancient times. The great Athenian fifth-century B.C. tragedians Sophocles, Euripides, and Aeschylus, for example, based their plays on tales about King Oedipus, Jason and Medea, and others that were as old in their day as Chaucer is in our day. The Roman poet Ovid collected and poetically retold the numerous fables and legends, Homeric and pre-Homeric, in a brilliant, interconnected tapestry called *The Metamorphoses* (A.D. 8). This work has served as an inspiration for the greatest writers in literary history, including Dante, Chaucer, Spenser, Shakespeare, Dryden, Pope, Racine, Keats, and Shelley, as well as the great modern writers James Joyce, Albert Camus, John Updike, Doris Lessing, and Margaret Atwood. So insightful of the complexities of the human psyche were these myths that the pioneers of modern psychoanalysis, Sigmund Freud and Carl Jung, based many of their theories on them (Freud's Oedipus and Electra complexes; Jung's archetypes, for example). (The word *psyche*, by the way, comes from the name of the mortal Psyche in the Roman tale of "Cupid and Psyche."[3])

What underlies the fascination with these ancient tales? In essence, their desire to satisfy our appetite for adventure, to venture into the unknown. It is their *universality*: In them, we recognize our deepest longings, our fears and weaknesses, our irrational impulses, and our insatiable craving for power and glory.

The ancient myths, then, remain a wellspring of potential possibilities for adaptation—either by elaborating on the original story in an original manner, including rendering the story as a stage play or film (think of *Clash of the Titans* or *My Fair Lady*—the musical adaptation of George Bernard Shaw's play *Pygmalion*—which in turn is an adaptation of the myth of Pygmalion), or by recasting the story in a modern context (think of James Joyce's rendering of Homer's *Odyssey* in his 1922 novel, *Ulysses*). Look around and you will see modern-day counterparts of Echo, Sisyphus, Phaethon, Cassandra, Prometheus, Athena, and hundreds more, each of whom embodies some human quality or deficiency: Cassandra, with her ability to predict the future, but fated never to be believed; Echo, unable to speak her own words, but only those of another; Phaethon's insistence on driving the sun across the sky in his father Apollo's chariot, with disastrous consequences.

How does a writer go about turning one of these myths into a modern story? As with any act of creation, some of the process simply cannot be described, other than to say that the writer makes a few imaginative and intuitive leaps in the dark. For example, let's say you choose to work with the tale of Narcissus, punished by the gods (for his arrogance and vanity) by making him fall in love with the first person he sees, which turns out to be himself, reflected in a pool). Your intuitive leap might be to recast Narcissus as a modern-day jewelry salesman whose self-love (i.e., *narcissism*) renders him utterly incapable of forming any kind of meaningful romantic relationship.

But let's slow down a bit and approach this story transformation process by adapting the steps presented in Chapters 3 through 8.

STEP 1: READ TWO OR THREE RETELLINGS OF THE MYTH IN QUESTION.

Dozens of mythologists, fiction writers, poets, and dramatists, enchanted by these ancient tales, have retold the myths in their own way. I recommend, among relatively modern mythologists, Thomas Bulfinch (*The Age of Fable*); Robert Graves (*The Greek Myths*); Edith Hamilton (*Mythology*); Norma Goodrich (*Ancient Myths*); Lucia Impelluso (*Myths: Tales of the Greek and Roman Gods*, in which the myths are categorized into Olympian Gods, Deities of Fate, Sea and Water Deities, Earth Deities, Infernal Deities, Monsters, and so forth, and in which each myth is illustrated with a famous painting or sculpture depicting the hero); and Arthur Cotterell (*World Mythology*, which includes illustrated summaries of the great myths from the Ancient Near East, Egypt, India, the Celts, Oceanus, China, Japan, Africa, and the Native Americas).

Why read more than one retelling? Doing so will give you a greater sense of the story possibilities that a given myth can generate. One mythologist might emphasize immediate events; another may think more in terms of long-term consequences; still another may focus on the personalities of the characters or the dynamics of their interactions. All of these approaches are valid; you might look for ways to combine them or for ways to take an entirely new approach.

STEP 2: FREE-ASSOCIATE ABOUT THE MYTH.

Write down whatever comes to mind when you think about the myth in question. Remember that myths, to use Jung's term, are *archetypes*: They manage to render concretely and dramatically, subtle facets of the human condition. Thus, if you choose to work with the myth of Narcissus, a tale that captures the tragic consequences of self-love, you might come up with something like this:

People get what they deserve! Self-centered people who are unable or unwilling to consider the feelings of others are destined to be ignored or scorned. How is it possible that such people wind up in relationships yet are never concerned about whether those close to them are unhappy or in pain or frustrated or angry? They seem to live in a bubble. The gods punished Narcissus for his insensitivity toward Echo (or toward anyone else), but the punishment—falling in love with his own reflection, with himself—is in a sense redundant. Narcissus is his own worst enemy; it is his *behavior* that winds up being his punishment. Behavior is destiny. It doesn't have to be that way, though, does it? Can a person with narcissistic tendencies, or even a total narcissist, break free of this kind of blindness? That's what it is: emotional blindness. I wonder what it would take to cure a narcissist. Maybe narcissism is an addiction like alcoholism.

Note how this writer is probing the psychological aspects of Narcissus's behavior and is beginning to wonder about whether that behavior (in this case self-centeredness resulting in insensitivity toward other people's needs and feelings) is indeed destiny. Such skepticism may lead the writer toward working up a modern-day retelling of the Narcissus myth.

STEP 3: GENERATE POSSIBLE STORY IDEAS OUT OF THE BLUE.
To begin thinking about "translating" the myth into a modern story, or using the mythological character as a springboard for a modern hero or anti-hero, do the following:

1. List possible story situations.
2. Create character profiles.
3. Map out possible connections from one event to another.
4. Draw a few trial scenes (or create collages using visuals from magazines and newspapers).

Start with your free associations from Step 1. For example, take the sentence "Behavior is destiny" from the free association passage in Step 1. Now pose these questions:

- Conjure up a situation in which a self-centered person misses an opportunity to form a relationship with a potential soul mate. In what social milieu do you want this drama to take place? In a workplace you're familiar with? In an athletic context? Your "conjuring" notes might begin like this:

  > During a skiing outing protagonist Lorie, a nurse, notices that her boyfriend, Gus, (a gifted but self-centered athlete) is limping in a way that suggests a torn knee tendon; but Gus insists he didn't become the terrific skier he is by caving in every time he experienced a slight injury. To complicate matters, Gus had hired a crew to capture his skiing prowess on film. With the film crew assembled, he executes what he hopes is a death-defying maneuver—and wipes out, severely injuring both legs. Instead of letting Lorie administer first aid, however, he screams at her for jinxing him with her overprotectiveness and ruining his chances of sports-film stardom.

- Now think in terms of depth of character. Using the character data sheet template from Chapter 4, write down details about Lorie's and Gus's physical and behavioral attributes. (Reminder: Do not use names or occupations or any other giveaway attributes of actual individuals. You do not want to be sued for slander! Better to exaggerate those attributes for literary effect anyway.)

STEP 4: PREPARE A MYTH-TO-STORY WORKSHEET.

After you've free-associated about the myth and generated possible story ideas out of the blue, it is time to think more methodically about how the "translation" process will pan out. This calls for filling out a myth-to-story worksheet like the following:

MYTH-TO-STORY WORKSHEET

I. Summarize the original myth in one paragraph: _____

_____

_____

_____

II. Explain what intrigues you most about the myth: _____

_____

_____

_____

III. In a separate paragraph transpose the myth into the modern world. What will change? What will stay the same?_____

_____

_____

_____

IV. Profile each of the principal characters in your story (you may want to prepare separate worksheets for this). Consider including comparisons between each character and his or her mythological counterpart._____

_____

_____

_____

V. State the premise of your myth-inspired story in a single sentence._____

_____

_____

_____

VI. What lasting theme do you want your story to convey? Is it the same as that of the original myth? Is it different? _____

_____

_____

_____

STEP 5A: PREPARE AN OUTLINE.

Once you have a general idea for a myth-inspired story, it is time to work out the story skeleton. Begin with a scratch outline, and then expand that scratch outline into a detailed outline, using the template that appears in Chapter 4.

If you were to go with the Lorie and Gus story, a portion of your outline might look like this:

I. Lorie (a nurse) is persuaded by her boyfriend Gus (a gifted but callous athlete) to accompany him on a hot-dogging skiing adventure.

    a. Lorie is hesitant; she hasn't known Gus that long.

    b. Gus shows Lorie his skiing trophies and photographs taken during several competitions; he also insists he can become an Olympic champ and plans to hire a camera crew to film his skiing prowess.

    c. She paradoxically admires and is repulsed by Gus's arrogance and superiority complex.

    d. She agrees to go, convincing herself that anyone as gutsy as Gus ought to have a trained nurse on standby.

II. Once at the ski resort, Gus pokes fun at the other skiers and even pokes fun at Lorie for being so cautious.

    a. Lorie tries to explain that her brother once suffered a near-fatal skiing accident by being reckless on the slopes.

    b. Gus accuses Lorie of insinuating that he, Gus, is a reckless skier.

III. Gus prepares for a skiing maneuver to convince Lorie of his skill. His camcorder buddies are ready to film the event.

    a. He wipes out.

    b. Lorie administers first aid on his badly injured legs.

    c. Instead of being grateful for her assistance, Gus accuses her of causing him to lose confidence and wipe out.

>   d. Lorie now realizes that Gus's narcissism is more serious than his knee injury, and she is determined to break off their relationship as soon as possible.
> IV. Lorie later tells Gus that she doesn't think they can have a healthy relationship. Gus retaliates by threatening to tell her hospital supervisor of her unorthodox nursing practices unless she sleeps with him.

One easy way to begin an outline is to copy the original free-association exercise and then tweak the sentences into causal and temporal order, adding and rearranging material as you go along.

STEP 5B: PREPARE A SYNOPSIS.

To reinforce the coherence of your story idea, summarize the key events in a concise manner, emphasizing how one event leads to another. A synopsis for the Lorie and Gus story might look like this:

> Lorie, a trained nurse, finds herself attracted to Gus, a suave, handsome athlete. He goes through the typical motions of dazzling her with his athletic accomplishments—this in the way of preamble to his asking her to accompany him on a hot-dogging skiing adventure. Lorie is both charmed and repulsed by his forwardness. She also begins to suspect that he is a narcissist (especially when she learns he hired a film crew), interested only in gratifying his own desires, and not the least bit interested in her interests. Still, she cannot help but admire his athletic prowess, wishing that she herself had the gumption to do daring things like skiing down steep slopes. At the ski resort, though, her cautious nature prevails, despite Gus's efforts to intimidate her. After he severely injures himself when showing off his hot-dogging skill, she rushes to his aid; but instead of expressing gratitude for her assistance, he accuses her not only of jinxing him with her "excessive" safety concerns, but with making his knee even worse. When Lorie decides she's had enough of this narcis-

sistic boor, he threatens to report her "botch job" on his knee to her supervisor—though all would be forgiven if she slept with him.

STEP 6: DO BACKGROUND RESEARCH (A) ON THE RELATIONSHIP BETWEEN MYTHOLOGY AND HUMAN BEHAVIOR; (B) ON THE MILIEU YOU'VE CHOSEN FOR YOUR MODERN RETELLING OF THE MYTH.

Here are some potentially useful sources:

- Scholarly commentary on the particular myth. The myth of Prometheus, for example, is analyzed by Carl Kerenyi in his book, *Prometheus: Archetypal Image of Human Existence*; the myth of Diana is analyzed by Pierre Klossowski in his book, *Diana at Her Bath*.
- Commentary on the significance of myths in general—e.g., Mircea Eliade, *Myth and Reality*.
- Information about the setting and activities associated with your modern retelling. For example, in the Lorie and Gus story, you would want do some in-depth reading about skiing maneuvers, competitions, dangers on the slopes, recommended safety precautions.

STEP 7: DRAFT THE STORY.

Once you've completed the above preparation, the actual drafting of the story should proceed smoothly. Avoid revising until you've completed the draft. When a sentence or paragraph does not feel right, type in a note to yourself to return to it after the draft is finished.

Before you start drafting, however, you may want to prepare another worksheet. We'll call this one a "Draft Management Worksheet." Its purpose is to prevent you from going off on a tangent and losing sight of the central purpose of your story idea. The next page contains one way to organize the worksheet:

DRAFT MANAGEMENT WORKSHEET

I. Title of the story:_____

II. What the story is about (one sentence): _____
_____
_____

III. Summary of the story (one paragraph): _____
_____
_____
_____

IV. Outline of the story (opening—middle/complication—ending/resolution)
_____
_____
_____

V. Character cast list, their physical and behavioral attributes:

    1. _____
       _____

    2. _____
       _____

    3. _____
       _____

    4. _____
       _____

    5. _____
       _____

ADAPTING THE MYTH
FOR A MODERN READERSHIP

Instead of using a myth as the foundation for a modern story, as James Joyce uses Homer's *Odyssey* as the foundation for his novel *Ulysses*, or as the writer of the Lorie and Gus skiing story uses the character of Narcissus as a springboard, you may wish to retell the myth in your own idiomatic manner. You may even wish to adapt it for the stage. Children's theater companies frequently stage fairy tales and myths for young audiences. To give you an example of how a myth can be adapted for the stage, I will compare a scene from the original *Cupid & Psyche* story by Apuleius with my own adaptation of it for the stage.

Here is Apuleius's version:

> "Psyche!" Venus cried in a fury of indignation, "Surely he [Venus's son, Cupid] hasn't picked out Psyche, the pretender to my throne of beauty, the rival of my renown! And, insult added to injury, he has taken me as a bawd, for it was my finger that pointed the way to the trollop." With this complaint she rose up out of the sea and hurried to her Golden Chamber, where she found her sick son, just as she had been told. Before she was through the door, she began yelling at him. "Fine goings-on! So perfectly in accord with our position in the scheme of things and your good name! First of all, you trample on the express orders of your mother—your queen I should say. Next, you refuse to stretch my enemy on the cross of dirty embraces. More, at your age you, a mere boy, entangle yourself in a low lewd schoolboy affair—just to annoy me with a woman I hate for daughter-in-law.[5]

And here is how I adapted the scene in my play, *Cupid and Psyche*:

VENUS (to a SLAVE): Summon my son to me.

141

SLAVE: He is still very weak from the oil burn [caused by Psyche's forbidden attempt to behold him, a god, with her own eyes].

VENUS: *Summon him!*

SLAVE (Stumbling to her feet): Y-Yes, Exalted One! (*Runs off*)

VENUS (Impatient for CUPID to enter): How could he have slandered me with such a deed? I am his mother. (CUPID enters, weakly) Look at you! You are no son of mine. The forests are filled with nymphs, but no! you had to dally among the humans—and to add insult to injury, get mixed up with the very one who has dared to rob me of my worshippers.

CUPID: It was an accident, Mother.[6]

The ancient myths and legends offer writers endless opportunities for story ideas. They can also help you break through writer's block (see Chapter 8). Simply read one of the myths as retold, say, by Thomas Bulfinch, and begin brainstorming for ways to recast the story in a modern context.

FOR YOUR WRITER'S NOTEBOOK

1. One of the most important sources of myth-based tales is the ancient Roman writer Ovid, whose *Metamorphoses* (ca. A.D. 8) has proven to be a valuable resource for writers since the Middle Ages. Read the following tales from this work; for each, come up with a scenario that places the story in a modern-day context.

   a. Phaethon's Ride [Book II], which tells of Apollo's son's insistence on driving his father's sun-chariot across the sky—with disastrous results.

    b. Arachne [Book VI], who asserted that her weaving skills were superior to Athena's, and was turned into a spider as punishment.

    c. Orpheus and Eurydice [Book X], the story of a gifted musician (Orpheus), whose lyre playing could soothe even savage beasts. After his beloved Eurydice died, he followed her into the Underworld and attempted to rescue her. Pluto consented to restore her provided Orpheus never look back to see if she were following him out of the Underworld. Alas, he failed to keep his promise and lost Eurydice forever.

2. Brainstorm for possible story ideas using the following mythological figures and their deeds as prompts. Consult a dictionary of mythology for additional prompts.

- **Albuna:** A nymph who had the gift of prophecy
- **Anchises:** A handsome Trojan prince with whom Aphrodite fell in love and bore his child, Aeneas, founder of the Roman race
- **Bellerophon:** A destroyer of monsters; died trying to fly to heaven on Pegasus, the winged horse
- **Delphi:** The site where the legendary oracle foretold the future
- **Hephaestus (Roman name: Vulcan):** The deformed blacksmith, son of Zeus, patron of artists, who created the arms of Achilles and Aeneas
- **Momus:** A god whose role it was to criticize and mock the other gods
- **Penelope:** The wife of Odysseus, who remained faithful throughout her husband's 20-year absence

- **Semele:** A mortal whose love affair with Zeus led to the birth of Dionysus, the god of wine and fertility

3. One of the most important sources of Hindu mythology is that of the Vedas, which tells of the supreme deity and his three attributes, Creation (Brahma), Preservation (Vishnu), and Destruction (Siva). After reading about these three personified powers, suggest a fantasy tale in which you give these powers human form.
   - **Brahma:** Creator of the universe; the human soul is one manifestation of him
   - **Vishnu:** Descended to earth in various manifestations (avatars), such as Manu (ancestor of the human race)
   - **Siva:** The counterforce of creation, whereby all things must come to an end

4. Four of the best-known myths today are those of Cassandra, Prometheus, Pygmalion, and Sisyphus. After reading the summaries of each myth below, generate a story idea, set in the modern world, in which each mythological hero (or anti-hero) is the main character.
   - **Cassandra:** Apollo, who had fallen in love with her, promised her the gift of prophecy provided she submit to his passion. When she refused, Apollo (unable to revoke the gift) made it so that her prophecies would never be believed.
   - **Prometheus:** He accused the gods of deceit and stole fire from them. As punishment for that crime, Zeus ordered him chained to a rock where vultures would feast on his liver (which grew back the next day) for 30 years. After being freed, he gave humankind the stolen fire and taught them the art of agriculture and medicine.

- **Pygmalion:** A king of Cyprus, he became a famous sculptor. Unable to form relationships with women, he created a statue of a woman that was so beautiful he fell in love with it—and then begged Aphrodite to give it life. His wish was granted, and the statue became the woman Galatea, whom Pygmalion married.
- **Sisyphus:** For violating his brother's daughter, he was ordered, in death, to roll a boulder to the top of a hill only for it to roll back down, only for him to roll it back up again, and so on through eternity.

CHAPTER 11

Creating a Short Story From a Newspaper Report

Newspapers always excite curiosity.

—CHARLES LAMB, *DETACHED THOUGHTS ON BOOKS AND READING*

Stories are about people facing an urgent problem: a threat to their reputation, their identity, their security (or a loved one's security). We enjoy stories because we enjoy learning about the different ways in which people, real or fictional, manage to solve such problems. Stories dramatize the problems that we ourselves could possibly face.

Newspapers are an ideal resource for timely, true stories about people around the world (as well as in our own communities) confronting problems of all sorts. Fiction writers often scour their daily newspaper for ideas. However, writers unfamiliar with the process of transforming a raw idea into a finished story need to know specifically how the process works. In this chapter, I will take you through that process—one that I have broken down into eight steps:

First, a preliminary step—not so much a step as it is a kind of mental readiness or receptivity, necessary for the idea-recognition process: *Read the newspaper article with a writer's eye.* We generally read news stories strictly for their information content, not as potential seed bearers of short stories or novels. With human-interest features, we might imagine what it would be like if we were in the situation being described; but even here we don't usually imagine expanding the situation into a full-fledged work of fiction.

However, if you are intent on working up story ideas based on articles from the daily newspaper (or from weekly news magazines such as *U.S. News & World Report* or monthly public affairs magazines such as *The Atlantic*, or other kinds of issues-oriented periodicals, for that matter), you need to read like a writer.

What does it mean to read with a writer's eye? How is it different from ordinary reading? Basically, it means asking questions about the writing itself:

- Why did the writer decide to open with that particular fact or anecdote or question? Would an alternative opening have been more effective?
- What was the writer's motive for choosing this figure of speech or that analogy or that example to illustrate his or her point?
- What might the writer have omitted from, or slighted in, the article?
- Why did the writer organize the article in the manner presented?

The purpose of reading with a writer's eye is to better understand and appreciate the rhetorical choices (and there are always choices) the writer has made to create an effective feature. To read like a writer, then, is to read for technique, not just for content.

Now then, let's proceed to the article-to-story-idea process:

1. Apply the "what if" question to different aspects of the article.
2. Brainstorm about the people mentioned in the article.
3. Apply the "so what" question to the article.

4. State your story idea in one sentence.

5. Free-associate about your story.

6. Prepare a rough outline or synopsis of your story.

7. Do the necessary background research to fill in the information gaps that the article does not cover or only touches upon.

8. Draft the story.

STEP 1: APPLY THE "WHAT IF" QUESTION TO DIFFERENT ASPECTS OF THE ARTICLE.

Seldom will a newspaper article suggest a story right off the bat. You may need to deploy your writer's imagination (which is already in high gear if you've been making use of this book so far). The "what if" question could prove to be your most versatile tool for turning an ephemeral news report into a page turner of a short story or even a novel. Today, as I write, I am looking over a report about radioactivity hazards from abandoned uranium mines on Navajo land in Utah, Arizona, and New Mexico—the result, according to the *New York Times* reporter Leslie Macmillan, of "shoddy mining practices and federal neglect" from the 1940s through the 1980s. Navaho residents had been consuming contaminated well water and breathing in radioactive dust all that time, resulting in outbreaks of cancer and other afflictions.

Potential material for a story? Yes indeed, but the "what if" question is needed to produce a sharply focused conflict situation:

- *What if* a Navajo leader decided to sue the federal government (specifically the Department of the Interior) for gross negligence?
- *What if* Navajo prospectors discovered a vast new source of uranium (or other militarily valuable elements) on their land but refused to allow federal access to it unless the contaminated areas were cleaned up (at a cost, some estimate, at several hundred million dollars)?
- *What if* EPA inspectors discovered that underground water contaminated by radioactive waste had penetrated waterways

feeding major metropolitan areas like Phoenix, Tucson, and Albuquerque?

- *What if* the radioactivity in the water had altered the genetic makeup of those drinking it, causing them to have unusual impulses or even giving them special powers?

STEP 2: BRAINSTORM ABOUT THE PEOPLE MENTIONED IN THE ARTICLE.

Every news story involves people in some way, directly or indirectly; this is the *who* element of the journalist's who-what-where-when-and-why heuristic. The human element is a basic ingredient in reportage because people are always behind the things that matter and contribute to the purpose underlying any story. Even nontechnical science articles call attention to the scientists behind the new discovery or controversial experiment.

Leafing through my files of newspaper clippings (I have enough clippings, in dozens of categories, to trigger ten lifetimes' worth of story ideas), I pause at a story published in *The New York Times* (March 15, 2012) about a zoologist researching the bite force of crocodiles. Most readers would probably regard the feature as an amusing trifle; but if you're a writer scouting for ideas, you would likely find it rich in story possibilities, thanks in part to the information given about the scientist, Greg Erickson, a professor at Florida State University with a specialty in biomechanics. Dr. Erickson's research has revealed that a crocodile's bite force increases with the animal's size, not the proportions of head and snout as earlier assumed. Now it's possible that a writer scouting for story ideas might see a story possibility there—perhaps a mystery story in which the force of a crocodile's bite helps a forensic specialist determine the cause of a victim's death—but I see something different, a story involving the making of a crocodile scientist. What experiences led to the fictional scientist's fascination with crocodiles? This root question triggers a list of subordinate questions:

- What kinds of high school and/or college biology teachers did he have? How did they inspire him?
- What made crocodiles or alligators, of all creatures, particularly fascinating to him?
- Which movies or TV documentaries, if any, kindled his fascination with crocodiles?
- What books did he read that enhanced his knowledge of crocodiles?
- Did he have any firsthand experience with a crocodile? What kind?

In answering these and any other questions that leap to mind, don't just be logical, be imaginative! For example, with regard to the last question, you might give your scientist protagonist a traumatic adolescent experience whereby some high-school buddy of his bets him five dollars for every minute he would wade in a river where alligators frequently appear. He foolishly takes the bet, wades in the river for five minutes, and wins twenty-five dollars.

All right, you say, but there's not much of a story in that. True! This brings us to Step 3.

STEP 3: APPLY THE "SO WHAT" QUESTION TO THE ARTICLE.
This question tests whether the story has larger significance than just "today's news." Is there a timeless theme behind it? Not every newspaper article will strike you as having thematic possibilities. Be careful not to give up too quickly on a news story, however. Remember the "what if" question that can help you tweak the original article to produce a more distinctive conflict situation, which in turn can be given thematic significance via the "so what" question.

Let's put this question to the test. Once again rummaging through my files of clippings, I come upon an article from *The Wall Street Journal* on the demise of handwriting instruction in public schools (Theodore Dalrymple, "The Handwriting Is on the Wall," WSJ July 9–11,

2011). What instigated the story was the announcement by Indiana state officials that schools in their state would no longer be required to teach handwriting to children because kids are doing all their writing on electronic devices.

"So what?" you ask.

First go back to "what if?" What if the time came when children (or adults) no longer were able to write in longhand? What are some possible consequences?

- Children (and eventually adults), deprived of the physical sensation of writing by hand (shaping words on the page; transmitting thoughts with quality ink on quality paper), would be missing out on an important dimension of person-to-person communication.
- Letters and greetings would lose their intimacy.
- People would cease to value handwritten documents—a significant cultural loss.

Now it becomes easier to answer "so what?" For example, if people were no longer capable of writing in longhand, the art of letter writing would disappear—yet another means of connecting with people in an intimate way across distances would be lost. (So what? you persist; we talk to each other on phones. Isn't that at least as intimate as writing to someone? Yes, of course—but a telephone voice is short-lived; once it stops, no record of it remains (unless it was recorded). Your challenge, if you were to pursue this premise in a work of fiction, would be to show dramatically why such a loss would be significant. Perhaps you would want to show that the more we depend upon electronic means of communication, the less capable we become in using language to transmit our most intimate thoughts and feelings.

STEP 4: STATE YOUR STORY IDEA IN ONE SENTENCE.
Always be able to answer the question, "What is your story about?" clearly and succinctly, ideally in one sentence. Why is this important?

Well, it means that you have a sufficient grasp of the foundation of your story—the bedrock on which you will unfold the story events. If you are unable to state the premise bluntly, you may not yet *have* a story to tell. That's fine—you just need to do some more brainstorming for basic ideas instead of plunging ahead in the dark. Sure, you may find your way eventually, but you'll waste a lot of time in the process.

I suggest that you practice capturing the premises of stories you know in a single sentence. For example, "Shirley Jackson's 'The Lottery' is a story about the barbaric acts that a farming community of otherwise ordinary people are capable of committing when their judgment is ruled by superstition and fear."

Also, that single-sentence statement of your story's central purpose will serve as a useful beacon as you develop the story, helping you to stay on track.

STEP 5: WRITE SPONTANEOUSLY (FREE-ASSOCIATE) ABOUT YOUR IDEA.

Using the strategies that I described in Chapter 4, let your imagination work its magic on your newly conceived story idea. You may come up with relevant content you might otherwise have overlooked if you had skipped this step and proceeded directly to outlining. Perhaps you've come up with a story idea involving a Navajo farmer who seeks reparations from the government for the damage to his land, and to the health of his family and his people, caused by radioactive waste from uranium mining. Part of your freewrite might read like this:

> When Tom Eagle was told that there was nothing the government could do, under existing laws, to clean up the radioactive waste from his land and from the reservation's water supply, he refused to be brushed off. This was simply too critical a problem and too great an injustice, the latest of a long line of injustices done to his people going back a century and a half. But how to proceed? He needed to search for possible loopholes in the existing laws. (You

could make one of the characters an attorney with a specialty in Indian affairs; together the two of them figure out
a plan—but time is running out because more and more of
his people are getting sick from the contamination, including his children.)

STEP 6: PREPARE A PRELIMINARY OUTLINE OR SYNOPSIS OF YOUR STORY.

Using the methods for constructing an outline or synopsis presented in Chapter 6, work out the beginning (opening conflict situation),
middle (complication), and ending (resolution) for your story. Remember that outlining is a heuristic device, a quick way to generate content and structure.

Begin the outline by restating the premise of your story. If you want
to write a story about a Navajo farmer who wishes to put an end to the
government's refusal to clean up the radioactive waste from uranium
mining on their land, you might state your premise like this:

> A Navajo farmer sues the federal government for gross neg-
> ligence in refusing to clean up radioactive contamination
> from uranium mining on Navajo land.

Next, for the "Beginning," state the conflict situation, using your one-
sentence premise as a springboard:

> I. When Tom Eagle learns that the groundwater and soil
> on his farm (and elsewhere on Navajo land) has been con-
> taminated by radioactive runoff from uranium mining, he
> requests a federal cleanup, but to no avail.

Before proceeding to the "Middle and Ending," you might want to
break down this Beginning into subordinate segments. For example:

> 1A: An agent from the Department of the Interior visits
> Tom Eagle's farm and offers a cash settlement under the

Radiation Exposure Compensation Act, but Tom insists that it is far from sufficient.

1B: The agent says there are no provisions for cleaning up the land. The only thing the government can do under the existing law is to offer a cash settlement.

1C: Tom decides to file a lawsuit on grounds that the U.S. government failed to meet its obligations. He demands additional compensation to enable him and his family to resettle on uncontaminated land.

It might be prudent, though, to work out the Middle and Ending first before adding subordinate elements.

Next, for the "Middle" segment of your preliminary outline, conceive of one or more compelling complications to the conflict. Maybe something like this:

II. When Tom's wife and child show symptoms of radiation sickness, Tom decides to take drastic action. Moreover, he learns of cancer outbreaks throughout the reservation. Knowing he cannot act alone, he hires an attorney with an excellent track record in winning compensation for Native American causes. Further complication: The attorney's reputation has been compromised by an arrest for assault during a protest demonstration years ago.

And finally, under "Ending," describe how the conflict will be resolved.

III. Tom's attorney proves that he still has clout by recruiting activists from a dozen other Native American reservations across three states, where contamination from uranium mining has caused widespread sickness and death. His activism, with Tom's help, leads to the largest government cleanup operation in history, along with complete medical coverage for victims of radioactive contamination.

Of course, you will most likely change your mind about the plot once you begin drafting the story. The point of outlining is to figure out a way to proceed. If you get a new idea, say about the conflict, adjust your outline accordingly. For example, you might decide to enhance the contamination threat by having Tom Eagle discover (through a close friend outside the reservation, maybe) the existence of a conspiracy to falsify an EPA report on the severity of the radioactive waste.

STEP 7: DO THE NECESSARY BACKGROUND RESEARCH TO FILL IN THE INFORMATION GAPS THAT THE ARTICLE DOES NOT COVER OR ONLY TOUCHES UPON.

Many a story falls flat because the writer did not re-create the story milieu in sufficient detail simply because he or she was unfamiliar with it. Familiarity comes either from extensive firsthand experience with the milieu or from thorough research—preferably both. You will want to review Chapter 7 for pointers on how to conduct background research if you are not already familiar with the process. Remember that research involves not just looking up facts or even reading books on the subject in question, but tracking down primary sources—government documents relating, say, to uranium mining and on the resulting radioactive waste; or hospital records documenting treatment of radiation victims; or legal documents covering earlier cases involving the Radiation Exposure Compensation Act, if you were to pursue the story about Tom Eagle and his plight.

STEP 8: DRAFT THE STORY.

The novelist William Styron once characterized writing (i.e., drafting) as "a form of self-flagellation." It takes a great deal of self-discipline to eke out sentence after sentence, paragraph after paragraph, page after page, for days and weeks and even months if you're writing a book. But the pleasures of writing outshine the pain of writing. So forget about what Styron said; think instead of novelist Rebecca West's reason for writing: to find out about things.

Assuming that you have tended to the preceding steps, drafting your story should proceed relatively smoothly. That's because you already know your story's premise, the characters, and the plot structure. But in unfolding the story, think less about structure or direction (you have your notes and outline for that), and more about creating dramatic immediacy. Think sensory description; think about making your characters seem like flesh-and-blood human beings.

FOR YOUR WRITER'S NOTEBOOK

1. Locate five newspaper articles. If you subscribe to the online versions, print out these five stories, along with accompanying photographs (photos will often suggest possibilities for settings and characters). For each article prepare the following:
    - A summary of the article
    - Three or more "what if" questions and your answers to them
    - A one-sentence response to the "so what" question
    - A one-sentence statement of a story premise derived from each article
2. Take one of the five story premises you conjured up in #1 above and construct a tentative three-part outline or synopsis: Beginning, Middle, Ending.
3. Develop a formal outline from the tentative outline you prepared in number 2 above.
4. Conjure up a story premise based on the following titles of news articles:
    - "Living with Pain: What Happens When you Can't Make it Go Away?" (by Claire Suddath; *Time*, March 7, 2011)
    - "Hello, Hal: Will We Ever Get a Computer We Can Really Talk To?" (by John Seabrook; *The New Yorker*, June 23, 2008)

- "Which Way to the Ball? I'll Ask My Gown" [Wearable electronics] (by Anne Eisenberg; *The New York Times*, February 26, 2012)
- "Britain Considers Electronic Surveillance Program" (by Raphael Satter; *San Francisco Chronicle*, April 2, 2012) [The British government is preparing proposals for a nationwide electronic surveillance network that could keep track of every message sent by any British citizen to anyone at any time.]

5. On March 15, 2012 *The New York Times* ran a full-page advertisement (a kind of infomercial) for the Museum of Modern Art in New York City. The ad consisted of eighteen or so reproductions of children's reactions to what impressed them in the museum, using cards with the words "I went to MoMA and . . ." Four children responded as follows:

- ". . . and fell deeply into pools of color."
- ". . . and I must go home and make art."
- ". . . and [now] see my mother in a new way."
- ". . . and I washed my brain."

Conjure up a story about a child who visits an art museum and beholds a work of art that transforms his or her outlook on life.

6. It isn't necessary to rely on just one newspaper article for a story idea. Think about imaginatively combining two unrelated articles in order to generate a story idea. Here are a couple of examples:

- An article about an art dealer who rescues stone sculptures from demolished buildings (John Freeman Gill, "Ghosts of New York"; *The Atlantic*, June 2010) + an oped piece by Diane Ackerman on turning wastelands into parks ("Emerald Cities"; *The New York Times*, August 16,

2011) = a story about how a homeless person gathers discarded art objects from trash piles and transforms a vacant lot into a weird sculpture garden.

- An article about a genetically engineered mosquito used to fight malaria (Stephen Ferris, "Building a Better Bug"; *The Atlantic*, October 2011) + an article on how animal intelligence (Virginia Morell, "Minds of Their Own"; *National Geographic*, March 2008) = a story about how a genetically engineered mosquito, originally designed to combat mosquito-borne diseases, mutates into one that attacks dogs and cats, causing them to revolt against their owners.

7. For those who are more accustomed to getting their news from online newspapers, visit the websites of your favorite newspapers and print out five news stories that strike your fancy. Follow the procedures suggested in number 1 through number 3 above to arrive at five story possibilities. Choose one of them to develop into a short story.

8. *The Huffington Post* has become one of the most widely accessed online newspapers in the country. Visit their website and locate one news story or feature from each of their categories (entertainment, sports, science, and so on). Use these articles as springboards for story ideas, following the suggestions given in prompts number 1 through number 3 above.

CHAPTER 12

Centering Your Memoir on Family Memorabilia

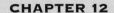

We have so much to remember these days. —ANNE LAMOTT

When it comes to memoir writing, one tends to assume that "getting an idea" doesn't apply or is redundant. Obviously, the rationale goes, the "idea" is your own life!

Well, yes and no. Yes in the sense that you will indeed be writing about events so familiar to you that they could practically write themselves; but no in the sense that a memoir ought to have an angle, built around a focal point, like any other narrative. The usual way to achieve that angle or focus is to select individuals, events, places, or objects in your life that can best represent your life story. But because you have so much to choose from, as Anne Lamott points out in her book, *Bird by Bird: Some Instructions on Writing and Life*—too much to choose from, perhaps—you need to be selective if you want your memoir to be coherent, enjoyable, and instructive. You don't want to clutter it with disconnected paraphernalia. It might represent the "real you," but it would make for rather turgid reading.

What I propose here is one approach out of many: Build your life story around key memorabilia; that is, material objects that have high sentimental and symbolic value for you, each object capable of embodying an incident or phase of your life.

Sounds good, you say; but how do I get going? I suggest the following steps:

1. Decide on a central theme for your memoir
2. Make a list of memorabilia that define you in some way
3. Write spontaneously about each object
4. Prepare a preliminary chapter-by-chapter outline/worksheet
5. Write a preliminary draft of one or more of the chapters
6. Do background research
7. Write the first draft of your memoir

Let's look closely at each of these steps:

STEP 1: DECIDE ON A CENTRAL THEME FOR YOUR MEMOIR.
Some memoirists start drafting segments of their life story before thinking seriously about theme and structure. Not a problem if you're convinced at the outset of how you want your memoir to develop; but doing some initial reflecting on theme and structure will save you time in the long run.

First of all, think about the way your life has changed over the years. What defined you best as a nine-year-old is not what defined you best as a fifteen-year-old or as a twenty-two-year-old. People have life-altering experiences, epiphanies, changes of fate. At the same time, ask yourself what values, convictions, impulses, and other foundational items have remained more-or-less constant even as your tastes, interests, and temperament have changed. It could even be the case that these "core" values and convictions were strengthened by your new interests and experiences. Here, then, is the key to determining a central theme for your memoir.

STEP 2: MAKE A LIST OF MEMORABILIA THAT DEFINE YOU IN SOME WAY.

Begin with your earliest memories. What toys did you enjoy when you were, say, four years old? Did you love a special doll that told you secrets? Perhaps you remember a colorful sand pail and shovel you took to the beach with you and used to create sand castles or collect seashells. What holiday or birthday gifts did you receive when you were eight or seventeen that made a lasting impression on you, and why? Try not to overlook anything. You might ask relatives to spur your memory; old photographs might help as well. Resist being selective at this point—you don't yet know what you'll want to incorporate or exclude from your life story until you begin drafting. The following prompt sheet may help you recall things:

MEMORABILIA PROMPT SHEET

(Separate sheet for each object)

Your age: _____

Type of object: _____

_____

_____

_____

Description of the object: _____

_____

_____

_____

How obtained: Gift/Award/Heirloom/Found object/Something I created __

_____

_____

If a gift, who gave it to you? _____

_____

_____

_____

_____

If an heirloom, from whom did you inherit it? _____

_____

_____

_____

_____

Significance that the object has for you: _____

_____

_____

_____

_____

Another way of generating content about memorabilia is to focus on individual years or stages of your life, and reflect on the objects associated with each stage. Use your notebook to jot down the things you recall owning or being fascinated by during early childhood, early and late adolescence, early adulthood, and so on. Almost inevitably, the significance that our possessions have for us changes as we move from one phase of our lives to another, so it's useful to record those changes.

Your list might look something like the following:

MEMORABILIA IN MY LIFE: CHILDHOOD YEARS

EARLY CHILDHOOD

My dog, Ludwig—

   —part Dachshund, part whatever; he loved taking me for a walk

Paintings of clowns—

   —hovered over my bed. I only pretended to like them. They always struck me as freakish rather than funny. Maybe it had something to do with that wild orange hair, the tomato nose, the oversize mouth that never changed expression.

Red ballerina slippers—

   —reminded me of Dorothy's ruby slippers

Stuffed animals—

   —tiger, teddy bear, giraffe . . . each one took me to different places while I was falling asleep

LATE CHILDHOOD

Stone angel in our backyard garden—

   —Why I associate gardening with spirituality even today.

Helium balloons—

   —Sparked my fascination with chemistry

Favorite Halloween costumes:

   —Superwoman, Betty Boop, Lily (from *The Munsters*)

A Hopi kachina doll that told me strange stories at night

STEP 3: WRITE SPONTANEOUSLY ABOUT EACH OBJECT.
You're not drafting part of your memoir at this stage but simply bringing long-dormant thoughts about this object to the surface. Associations you have with the object are important, so don't try to hold back on grounds that it isn't directly relevant. Writing spontaneously about stuff from your childhood and young adult years will help you to recall the special fascination these objects held for you, and even how they shaped your views about the world. For example, when I was a kid, one of my uncles gave me a printing set for a Christmas present. In writing about that gift I remind myself of the subtle influence it had on me.

> It was called a Printer's Kit. The cover of the sturdy box depicted a scene inside a printer's shop: one person setting type, another, wearing a black apron, feeding sheets of paper into a Platen press; another person gathering the sheets. The kit consisted of rubber type pieces—letters, punctuation marks, spaces, numbers, miscellaneous symbols; a tray for organizing the type, a 5- or 6-line holder for preparing the text; sheets of paper, and an ink pad. Ah, the pungent smell of printing ink! Maybe it was that ink, even more than the pieces of type with their inverted letters and numbers, that intrigued me: there was magic in how inked letters could make printed words. Was that the basis for my seeing magic in the way a handful of letters, arranged in different configurations, could produce hundreds of thousands of words, which in turn could produce an infinite number of texts?

Revisit these spontaneous writings from time to time; additional recollections may leap to mind when you do.

STEP 4: PREPARE A PRELIMINARY CHAPTER-BY-CHAPTER OUTLINE/WORKSHEET.
I emphasize "preliminary": Your initial efforts at determining a structure for your life story are trial and error. Some things won't fit where you first place them—but you won't be able to determine that until you

write it down. Unlike outlines for other writing projects, the outline for your memorabilia-centered memoir ought to include reference to the defining object.

Here is how a portion of the outline for one of your chapters might look:

> **Chapter_____**
> **Theme:** Discovering my love of chemistry
> **Representative Memorabilia:** Chemistry set Mom gave me for my twelfth birthday; guidebook of gems and minerals Literary allusions to be made (perhaps): Oliver Sacks, *Uncle Tungsten: Memories of a Chemical Boyhood* ("Many of my childhood memories are of metals: these seemed to exert a power on me from the start.")

[outline]

> I. My fascination with the different kinds of chemical elements
> II. Realization that ninety-two elements (not counting the radioactive ones) make up the entire earth, the entire universe
> III. Mixing chemicals: made me feel like a magician. (Later wondered if this was how the medieval alchemists felt)
> IV. Respect for dangerous chemicals—how carelessness can lead to serious accidents

STEP 5: WRITE A PRELIMINARY DRAFT OF ONE OR MORE OF THE CHAPTERS.

Again, I emphasize "preliminary" because you're mainly drafting to get the feel of how the narrative of your life should unfold. Do you want to sound serious? Nostalgic? Witty? Angry? Satirical or tongue in cheek? Maybe figure out a way of modulating from one tone to another?

Although a memoir may not be plotted like a novel, it still has to read like one. A memoir is a narrative, after all, a story that unfolds in time and space. Like a novel, a memoir can move in nonlinear fashion from present to past, and spatially, from city to city, from one special place to another.

STEP 6: DO BACKGROUND RESEARCH.

How, you may wonder, does one go about researching one's own life? Answer: By focusing almost exclusively on "primary" sources such as letters, diaries, direct conversations with friends and relatives. (See Chapter 7.) Your goal is to gather information outside of your experiences in order to give greater perspective on those experiences.

Suggestion: When interviewing or conversing informally with friends and family, prepare a set of questions to ask. Try to memorize them so that your interview doesn't seem like an interrogation. Here are a few sample questions:

- How did I react when you first gave me that [Erector Set, dollhouse, baseball bat, bicycle, or other prized possession]?
- When did my interests seem to change? What caused the change?
- How would you describe my temperament when I was [a certain age]?
- Was I outgoing? Did I like to play with other children? Was I moody? Obedient? Mischievous?

STEP 7: WRITE THE FIRST DRAFT OF YOUR MEMOIR.

As you're drafting your life's story, be sure to keep your readers firmly in mind: They don't know you, and it is your job to get them interested in you. Tone of voice is important: Avoid flat summary; instead, imagine that you are speaking to your readers around a table on a winter evening, a fire crackling in the hearth. Keep them intrigued not just with the events in your life, but with evocative language and dramatic immediacy. Note how Lauren Slater manages both tasks in the following passage from her memoir *Prozac Diary*, in which Slater expresses her fear that taking Prozac might cause her to lose her ability to write:

... the words felt dull, dead. A bright layer separated me from them, and as I sensed correctly at the time, the barrier would remain as a perpetual part of my Prozac career. That night I tried again and again. Calling. *Shhh.* Calling. *Shhh.* The air swirled. Something flapped and faded.

ADDITIONAL MEMOIR WRITING APPROACHES TO CONSIDER

Although I've suggested just one approach to writing a memoir, there are numerous other approaches, and I'd like to mention some of them here. The first is what might be called a themed memoir: a story in which you discover your ancestral roots; or a story in which you discover the depths of your faith; or a story in which you explore the influences that shaped your way of thinking. By the way, each of these can be the basis for a separate memoir. Poet-memoirist Patricia Hampl, for example, has published four themed memoirs. The first one (*A Romantic Education*), published when she was only in her thirties, focuses on discovering her Czech roots—and her identity—through an extended visit to her ancestral homeland; the second (*Virgin Time*) focuses on her quest to extend the limits of her Catholic upbringing by going on pilgrimages to spiritual places like Assisi and Lourdes; the third (*The Florist's Daughter*), focuses on her growing-up years in St. Paul, Minnesota; and the most recent (*I Could Tell You Stories: Sojourns in the Land of Memory*) is Hampl's portrait of the memoirist as a young woman, so to speak—interconnected essays that focus on her literary influences, especially the art of memoir. Hampl, who is Regents Professor of English at the University of Minnesota and the recipient of a MacArthur Fellowship, reminds us of the often latent stories about ourselves we can tap into, and which can be brought to the surface through numerous means: a conversation with a parent or sibling, chancing upon a long lost photograph, paying a visit to the town where your grandmother grew up, and so on.

Now, in case you might be thinking that your life isn't nearly as interesting as Patricia Hampl's, that you've done nothing spectacular and have not been treated for psychological disorders like Lauren Slater. Well, what if I were to tell you that someone published a successful memoir based on her experiences as a housecleaner?

I'm referring to Louise Rafkin's delightful memoir, *Other People's Dirt: A Housecleaner's Curious Adventures* (Algonquin Books, 1998). I recommend it to anyone wishing to write a memoir, especially to those who are convinced their lives aren't worth writing about.

Before I say more about Rafkin's memoir, I'd like you to imagine that this is the subject you have chosen for your memoir. Grab a sheet of notebook paper and jot down any ideas that come to mind when you think of earning a living as a housecleaner. Go ahead, take your time; I'll wait.

I'm guessing that you thought of more things to say about something so seemingly dull as housecleaning than you realized. Louise Rafkin gives us a clue in her title as to what she is up to. The "dirt" she discovers when cleaning other people's houses is more than what she mops up off the floor—as was the case with the home of a cat lover/cultist:

> There was an altar and chanting sheets and everywhere small slips of paper that read "I deserve success" and "I deserve wealth." Cat litter covered the upstairs like New Year's confetti; downstairs hundreds of cat statues were coated with veritable cat fur.

Rifkin's memoir is filled with scenes like that—snapshots of people from all walks of life seen from the perspective of a housecleaner.

FOR YOUR WRITER'S NOTEBOOK

1. Make a list of memorabilia from each phase of your life (early childhood, late childhood, early adolescence, late adoles-

cence, early adulthood). For each item you list, write a paragraph describing what that object meant to you at the time and what it means to you now.

2. Try coming up with suggestions for building a memoir around each of the following occupations. Be inventive!

   a. A food server at a truck stop
   b. A librarian
   c. A hospital orderly
   d. A bank guard
   e. A trash collector
   f. An automobile assembly-line worker
   g. A janitor employed by the Pentagon
   h. Someone who journeys to her ancestral home to find her roots

CHAPTER 13
Structuring Your Novel Around a Symbol or Event

She [Hester Prynne] felt or fancied . . . that the scarlet letter had endowed her with a new sense. She shuddered to believe, yet could not help believing, that it gave her a sympathetic knowledge of the hidden sin in other hearts.

—NATHANIEL HAWTHORNE, *THE SCARLET LETTER*

Most aspiring writers dream of writing and publishing a novel; it is the genre that comes to mind when we hear the word "author." After all, it is the genre that most often is scouted for film adaptation and fills racks in airport gift shops. Novels are what we think of when we think of *literature* (well, modern literature at least). But the task of structuring a four-hundred-page story can be intimidating. There are so many things to coordinate: characters, story line (often multilayered), pacing, historical or social milieu—no wonder many would-be novelists abandon their projects after a week or so.

While there are no shortcuts to novel writing, it is possible to get a novel under way with relative ease. In Chapter 12 we examined a method of building a memoir around memorabilia—objects from different phases of your life that signify your experiences, values, and ideas. The same principle can work in constructing a novel. That is, you can build your novel around one or more objects or events that remind your protagonist of what matters most to him or her. In Fitzgerald's *The Great Gatsby*, for example, the boat dock belonging to Daisy Buchanan, Jay Gatsby's lost love (she had married a wealthy person like herself), becomes a beacon of hope for Gatsby, a kind of license (green light = go) to pursue her with his newly acquired wealth (most likely from bootlegging), even after learning that Daisy had married. In Melville's *Moby-Dick*, the white whale comes to symbolize the unattainable mystery of life that Ahab desperately wishes to embrace. In Hawthorne's *The Scarlet Letter*, Hester Prynne is both victimized and empowered by that emblem of shame—the embroidered *A* for *Adulteress*—that she is forced to wear in public. She is victimized in that she cannot escape the social milieu in which her transgression has made her and Pearl (her illegitimate child with the clergyman Dimmesdale) embodiments of sinfulness. She's also liberated, in a sense, in that her transgression has strengthened her resolve to resist the sinister machinations of her corrupt husband Chillingworth and thereby preserve the humanity of Dimmesdale and their daughter.

Deciding on a symbol or central event of symbolic significance for your novel should not be difficult. After all, we are symbolists by nature: our dreams are richly symbolic; we use symbols to represent our nationality, our religion. Even our clothes, jewelry, or body ornamentation can have symbolic meaning. Symbols are important because they are concrete representations of complex values; for that reason, they permeate every culture, past and present. Think of the symbolism inherent in a circus, for example—an interconnected series of persons and events that represent our fantasies as well as our fears:

- Trapeze artist . . . Childhood desire to fly, to overcome gravity (or any other physical limitation); gracefulness in the face of danger
- Lions . . . A deadly beast under control (but barely)
- Elephants . . . A giant, exotic beast capable of fascinating skills: magical in a child's eyes
- Monkeys . . . Animals behaving so much like unruly children they make us laugh, while at the same time reminding us how much a part of the animal kingdom we are
- Clowns . . . Comic, strange, symbolizing the freedom to behave unconventionally; possessing a kind of negative power; enacting our alter egos
- Ringmaster . . . Like a parent: managerial, yet the harbinger of surprises and delights

Deciding on a central symbol or symbolic event for your novel is a good way to get your novel underway, as I will demonstrate in the following pages. By the way, an excellent sourcebook for symbols and their cultural functions is J.E. Cirlot's *A Dictionary of Symbols*.

AN EIGHT-STEP METHOD FOR GETTING YOUR SYMBOL-CENTERED NOVEL UNDERWAY

The trickiest part of writing a novel is working out a story line to be sustained for an average of four hundred manuscript pages. Here, then, my eight-step method for a novel in which a symbolic object, event, or combination of the two (like a circus) serves as the catalyst:

1. Write a single sentence that begins with the words "My novel is about . . ."
2. Create a list of possible symbols (objects or events).
3. Choose one object or event from the list and write spontaneously about it.
4. Write a preliminary outline for the story, keeping that central symbol in mind.
5. Prepare one-page profiles for each of your principal characters.
6. Do the necessary background research.
7. Prepare a detailed outline or chapter-by-chapter synopsis.
8. Draft the novel.

Let's now consider each step in detail.

STEP 1: WRITE A SINGLE SENTENCE THAT BEGINS WITH THE WORDS "MY NOVEL IS ABOUT . . ."

Because beginning writers find the length of a novel—or at least the length of time it generally takes to complete a novel—rather intimidating, their impulse is to include as much as they can. How else can they fill four hundred pages? But novels are as long as they need to be to tell a coherent, in-depth, absorbing story. To ensure your book stays focused—i.e., that every scene contributes to the main idea—you need to articulate that main idea and refer to it often. You might even want to tape it to your wall.

Here are five "my novel is about" statements to give you a sense of how to form your own statement:

- *My novel is about* the struggle between a successful businessman and his musically gifted son, who wants nothing to do with the world of business despite his father's well-intentioned efforts to prepare him for an economically secure career.

- *My novel is about* a female veteran in the Afghan war whose abilities are questioned and even ridiculed despite her excellent combat record.
- *My novel is about* a schoolteacher who can no longer tolerate the strictures imposed upon him (and his fellow teachers) by the school principal and the school board.
- *My novel is about* a marine biologist who tries to prevent an oil company from drilling offshore and thereby risking an already endangered ecosystem.
- *My novel is about* a homeless person who experiences disturbing visions, whose life changes dramatically after a stranger gives her a watercolor paint kit.

STEP 2: CREATE A LIST OF POSSIBLE SYMBOLS (OBJECTS OR EVENTS).

Once you've worked out a premise for your novel, the next order of business is to decide on possible symbols that could serve as a beacon to maintain focus and coherence in your story. For example, if you were to write a novel about a female war veteran's struggle for acceptance, you might give her a combat wound that would serve as a symbol of her courage and perhaps also of her vulnerability (think of *The Red Badge of Courage*, in which Stephen Crane uses this kind of symbolism). If you were to write a novel about a teacher struggling to improve the learning environment at his school, you might use a cracked blackboard or a broken window or a torn map of the world or the United States as a symbol of neglect. It is also possible to use a symbol ironically—a painting of a pristine coral reef hanging in the office of the petroleum company's CEO, for example.

STEP 3: CHOOSE ONE OBJECT OR EVENT FROM THE LIST AND WRITE SPONTANEOUSLY ABOUT IT.

Even though you may decide to include several symbolic objects or events in your novel, choosing one central symbol would strengthen coherence. Although Harper Lee uses several symbols in *To Kill a Mockingbird* (the closed shutters of the Radley house; the mad dog that Atticus shoots; the black-bound Bible that Tom Robinson swears on in court) she gives her classic novel a sharp focus with its central symbol of the mockingbird, which, as Atticus explains, sings its heart out for everyone to enjoy.

Imagine that you want to write a novel about a homeless woman who brings her visions and inner longings to life in paintings after a stranger gives her a set of watercolors. The watercolors themselves can serve as a collective symbol (each color representing something important in the woman's life); but you decide that the central symbol of the novel should be the object she first decides to paint, which is . . . what? Think about possibilities for a moment:

- A lily (symbolizing purity, femininity, spiritual transcendence)
- A lake (where she meditated, free from her overbearing parents)
- A farmhouse (her girlhood home)
- An ornate chest (long lost, containing valuable secret documents)
- A self-portrait (except that she is dressed in a nineteenth-century gown—an image of herself in a previous life?)

Let's say you decide to work with the ornate chest. Your spontaneous writing might look something like this:

> The chest's ornate exterior will symbolize the promise of riches buried inside. And what is inside? A rare manuscript? A book? A miniature painting? Maybe go with a portrait of a woman (?) by some seventeenth-century Flemish master, handed down in secret from generation to generation. But why was it hidden away? Maybe because the homeless woman's great-great grandfather had stolen it from someone who threatened to destroy it? Or better yet: valuable as the painting itself might be, its worth isn't the reason for

its having been hidden, but rather what is encrypted on the
back of the canvas—or within the portrait itself? (shades of
Dan Brown!)—except that the encryption, once deciphered,
reveals the identity of the woman in the painting.

As this bit of freewriting indicates, it is easy to generate story content
by focusing on a single object. Spontaneous writing also increases your
psychological involvement with the story you're trying to create. The
more involved you are, the more realistic your storytelling is likely to
be. Some compare authorship to acting several parts at once in a play.

**STEP 4: KEEPING THAT CENTRAL SYMBOL IN MIND, WRITE
A PRELIMINARY OUTLINE OR SYNOPSIS FOR THE STORY.**
Before attempting to outline your novel, I recommend writing an outline for a novel you've read recently. If the novel isn't fresh in your
mind, reread it before trying to outline it. The time will be well spent:
You are reading the book—and constructing the outline—as a novelist in training.

Let's use Ken Kesey's 1962 masterpiece, *One Flew over the Cuckoo's
Nest*, as a case in point.

> **Premise:** The treatment of mentally ill patients in the middle
> of the twentieth century made the patients worse, not bet-
> ter, due to a profound misunderstanding of the nature of
> mental illness.
>
> I. The narrator, Chief Bromden, an 8-foot Native Amer-
> ican suffering from schizophrenia, is made to feel
> "tiny" and he also believes he's about to be run over
> by a giant combine (an important symbol in the nov-
> el). Other patients ("Acutes," "Chronics," and so forth)
> are treated as social outcasts or as imbeciles. Setting,
> mood, and circumstance are established in the first
> two chapters.
>
> II. Main story line: A new patient, Randle Patrick Mc-
> Murphy, joins the group and is quickly branded as

belligerent. He is able to see through the clinically approved barbarity epitomized by Big Nurse Ratched (ironic counterpoint to Chief Bromden, who has been made to feel tiny, a warrior reduced to a broom). McMurphy takes matters into his own hands by treating his fellow patients like human beings with human needs. For instance, he demands to know what kinds of medication they're being required to swallow; this inevitably leads to a showdown between McMurphy and Big Nurse.

III. McMurphy loses the battle (you can't fight the Combine—Chief Bromden's private metaphor for the Establishment—single-handedly!); however, Chief Bromden, having been re-empowered by the now incapacitated (lobotomized) McMurphy, manages to break free.

Now follow suit by preparing a brief introduction/body/conclusion outline or synopsis for your own symbol-driven novel.

STEP 5: PREPARE ONE-PAGE PROFILES FOR EACH OF YOUR PRINCIPAL CHARACTERS.

For any kind of novel, but especially a novel shaped largely by symbols, you want to think about the values your characters represent, not just about their particular role in the story. Character profiles for a novel can be tricky because characters do change in the course of a long story. Try to account for as many of these changes as you can, keeping in mind that the characters may likely evolve in ways you can't anticipate at the outset.

Think carefully about the names you give your characters. This may seem like a trivial suggestion; however, names are the first indicator of symbolic allusion in any kind of literary work. Think, for example, of Willy LOMAN in Arthur Miller's *Death of a Salesman* (Miller wanted to write a tragedy of the common [i.e., lowly] man);

of Roger CHILLINGWORTH in Hawthorne's *The Scarlet Letter*; of Mr. M'CHOAKUMCHILD, the insensitive schoolteacher in Charles Dickens's *Hard Times*; of Ebenezer SCROOGE of Dickens's *A Christmas Carol*—a name that has become synonymous with tightwad; of MOONWATCHER, the perceptive and inventive proto-human in Arthur C. Clarke's *2001: A Space Odyssey*. A subtler example is that of Chief BROMDEN, a name that evokes the sound of thunder or brings to mind a warrior hero—but this Native American has been made to feel tiny, reduced to "Chief Broom" (a bitterly ironic inversion of boom?), in effect made to sweep away the dirt of his oppressors.

STEP 6: DO BACKGROUND RESEARCH.

It is difficult to overestimate the importance of research for any kind of novel you wish to write. Some novelists prefer to do their research as soon as they have the premise nailed. Others prefer to wait until after working out a detailed outline or chapter-by-chapter synopsis. I recommend the latter because you'll have a better sense of the kind of research you need to do. But I do not recommend putting off the research until you're well into a first draft. As Karen Wiesner points out, "It's very hard to write a story with huge holes in your own knowledge. It's essentially doing the work backwards and creating a considerable amount of extra work for yourself in the process" (*First Draft in 30 Days*).

To begin your research, determine ahead of time what kinds of information you need to obtain:

- Facts about a certain geographic location
- The kinds of tools or weapons used in a given occupation, and how they are used
- How certain kinds of machinery function
- Day-to-day routines in a given workplace
- Hazards workers face in a particular line of work

- Jargon used in a given profession

Next, divide your tasks into manageable segments; don't try to research everything at once.

STEP 7: PREPARE A DETAILED OUTLINE OR CHAPTER-BY-CHAPTER SYNOPSIS.

With a clear idea of the controlling symbol for your novel, together with your preliminary outline, character profiles, and research notes, you are now ready to stitch together the story line, stage by stage. Each stage will be a chapter that carries the story through its conflict situations toward a climactic resolution.

A good way to prepare for this step is to write a chapter-by-chapter synopsis of a short novel you've read recently or are presently reading. As soon as you finish reading each chapter, write a one-paragraph summary of it.

STEP 8: DRAFT THE NOVEL.

Unlike drafting a short story, drafting a novel does not—and perhaps should not—proceed in linear beginning-middle-ending fashion. Some experts recommend writing the ending first, then weaving back and forth from introductory scenes to middle scenes, thereby keeping better track of causal or temporal interconnections, even though your chapter-by-chapter outline is supposed to ensure this (it might if it's sufficiently detailed). The most important thing is to remain open to unanticipated opportunities for plot twists and turns. A sudden notion to bring in a new complication may require you to rewrite the opening segment. An insightful comment made by a character can lead you to add new material later on.

Experienced novelists will tell you that characters take on a life of their own. It's not an exaggeration: Having devoted considerable time to preparing character profiles and then showing them in action page after page, you will discover that to be consistent with the behaviors with which you've endowed them, they will need to say or do things you could not have anticipated during the outlining stage.

A useful tool when drafting is a Draft Management Worksheet, similar to the one I suggested for crafting a short story (see Chapter 11), but adapted for drafting a novel:

NOVEL DRAFT MANAGEMENT WORKSHEET

I. Working title for the novel: _____

II. What the novel is about (one sentence): _____
_____

III. Summary of the novel (one paragraph): _____
_____

IV. Central symbol(s) if any: _____
_____

V. Chapter-by-chapter summaries:

    Chapter 1: _____
    _____

    Chapter 2: _____
    _____

    Chapter 3: _____
    _____

    Chapter 4: _____
    _____

    Chapter 5: _____
    _____

Chapter 6: _____

_____

Chapter 7: _____

_____

Chapter 8: _____

_____

Chapter 9: _____

_____

Chapter 10: _____

_____

[etc.] _____

_____

VI. Character cast list, with physical and behavioral attributes (brief sketches here; more elaborate profiles on separate worksheets)

1. _____

_____

2. _____

_____

3. _____

_____

4. _____

_____

5. _____

_____

SUGGESTIONS FOR YOUR NOVEL'S OPENING

Although it is tempting to obsess over your opening in the first draft, you run the risk of never getting off the ground if you do. Better to write the most plausible opening and then return to it as things begin to take shape.

That said, there's no underestimating the importance of coming up with compelling ideas for an effective opening—effective in the sense that it has to grab and hold the reader's attention for the next several hundred pages. Besides that, it is difficult to generalize. Some novelists, like John Steinbeck in *The Grapes of Wrath*, will devote an entire opening chapter to setting alone. Here are the first three sentences:

> To the red country and part of the gray country of Oklahoma, the last rains came gently, and they did not cut the scarred earth. The plows crossed and recrossed the rivulet marks. The last rains lifted the corn quickly and scattered weed colonies and grass along the sides of the roads so that the gray country and the dark red country began to disappear under a green cover.

Steinbeck's tone is almost biblical—and I suspect that was intentional, as he seems to be combining naturalism with a kind of Old Testament chronicle of the exodus from doom to the Promised Land in telling the story of Oklahoma farmers, victimized by the catastrophic crop failure in the Dust Bowl, who migrated to California to survive.

Other writers will secure their readers' attention by using any or all of the following devices:

- Establish or hint at the dramatic situation
- Acquaint us with the narrator and other people in the story
- Get us wondering what is going to happen
- Delight us with clever, witty, or provocative language

Consider Jack Kerouac's character-driven opening for *On the Road* (1955), the signature literary work of the Beat Generation:

> I first met Dean not long after my wife and I split up. I had just gotten over a serious illness that I won't bother to talk about, except that it had something to do with the miserably weary split-up and my feeling that everything was dead. With the coming of Dean Moriarty began the part of my life you could call my life on the road.

Notice what Kerouac has included in these two opening sentences: The narrator's reason for taking a road trip (his marital predicament, the fact that he'd recovered from a serious illness) and a teaser about an important character in the novel, Dean Moriarty.

Now let's look at the opening of a very different kind of novel, Margaret Atwood's chilling and disturbing postapocalyptic *The Handmaid's Tale*. It is set in a near-future theocratic state called the Republic of Gilead in which the very rare fertile women are confined as chattel in order to produce offspring so that the human species may survive:

> We slept in what had once been the gymnasium. The floor was of varnished wood, with stripes and circles painted on it, for the games that were formerly played there; the hoops for the basketball nets were still in place, though the nets were gone.

The most captivating thing about these opening lines is their elegiac tone, the profound sense of loss and resignation one associates with defeat—in this case not only military defeat but cultural defeat. The emblem of athletic vigor—a basketball court— is now used for a very different, very unathletic purpose: a shelter for captive Handmaids, carefully protected from the deadly outside environment.

FOR YOUR WRITER'S NOTEBOOK

1. Suggest a premise for a story in which each of the following objects might serve as a central symbol:
   a. A vulture
   b. An egg
   c. A cave
   d. The Queen of Hearts
   e. A fire opal
   f. Old Faithful
   g. A swamp
   h. Wind chimes

2. Give each of the following symbols from existing literary works a new association:
   a. A monolith (in *2001: A Space Odyssey*, the Monolith symbolized an enigmatic alien intelligence that guided human destiny)
   b. A house (haunted house stories are numerous; what symbolic significance can you give to an old house?)
   c. A ring (symbolizing something other than marriage or the source of evil power, as in Tolkien's fantasy trilogy, *The Lord of the Rings*)
   d. A river (symbolizing something other than a conduit through life, as in Mark Twain's *Huckleberry Finn*)

3. Suggest ways in which the following commonplace household objects or locations might be used symbolically in a novel:
   a. Window shade
   b. Rocking chair
   c. Closet
   d. Basement storeroom

4. Invent the names, with symbolic potential, of two characters (protagonist and antagonist) for each of the following novels:
    a. A story, set in the antebellum South, about a secret abolitionist
    b. A story about a compulsive gambler
    c. A story about teachers at an inner-city high school
    d. A story about circus clowns who create new acts for themselves

5. Plan a novel about a laborer who strives to find dignity in his or her life through work. Consider these possible occupations for your protagonist:
    a. Welder
    b. Dock worker
    c. Truck driver or bus driver
    d. Nurse's aide
    e. Garage mechanic
    f. Airline baggage handler
    g. Bartender
    h. Telemarketer

An excellent source for firsthand accounts about job experiences is Studs Terkel's *Working*.

6. Love stories are often symbol rich. Cupid's arrow, moonlight, engagement rings, flowers of all kinds (especially roses, especially *red* roses), chocolates in heart-shaped boxes, are well-known examples. Write a premise for a love story in which you use unconventional love symbolism. In Tracy Chevalier's *Girl with a Pearl Earring*, for example, the pearl earring merges as a complex symbol of love, desire, anesthetic beauty, and so on.

7. What symbol(s) do you see emerging in the following opening segments of two classic novels?

a. Around quitting time, Tod Hackett heard a great din on the road outside his office. The groan of leather mingled with the jangle of iron and over all beat the tattoo of a thousand hooves. He hurried to the window.

 An army of cavalry and foot was passing. It moved like a mob, its lines broken, as though fleeing from some terrible defeat. The dolmans of the hussars, the heavy shakos of the guards, Hanoverian light horse, with their flat leather caps and flowing red plumes, were all jumbled together in bobbing disorder. . . .

 While he watched, a little fat man, wearing a cork sun-helmet, polo shirt and knickers, darted around the corner of the building in pursuit of the army.

 "Stage Nine—you bastards—Stage Nine!" he screamed through a small megaphone.

 —Nathanael West, *The Day of the Locust*

b. It was late in the evening when K. arrived. The village was deep in snow. The Castle hill was hidden, veiled in mist and darkness, nor was there even a glimmer of light to show that a castle was there. On the wooden bridge leading from the main road to the village, K. stood for a long time gazing into the illusory emptiness above him.

 Then he went on to find quarters for the night. The inn was still awake, and though the landlord could not provide a room and was upset by such a late and unexpected arrival, he was willing to let K. sleep on a bag of straw in the parlor.

 —Franz Kafka, *The Castle*

CHAPTER 14
Seventy-Five Seminal Ideas for Your Novel

*Sing to me of the man, Muse, the
man of twists and turns,
Driven time and again off course, once
he had plundered
The hallowed heights of Troy.*

—HOMER, *ODYSSEY*, BOOK I

In the preceding chapter I suggested a method of structuring your novel by focusing on symbols that can embody the central theme as well as subordinate or chapter-specific themes. In this chapter, I will introduce you to another method, one which generates story ideas from popular categories. Dozens of possible categories exist, but I've selected fifteen that seem especially well-suited for kindling the imagination of an aspiring novelist:

- The Adventures of X
- The Clash Between X and Y
- Confessions of X
- Contact With X
- The Curse (or Prophecy) of X
- Descent Into X
- Escape From X
- The Haunting of X
- Journey to X
- The Love Between X and Y
- The Mystery of X
- The Rise and Fall of X
- Revenge of X
- The Search for X
- The Secret of X

Like symbols, categories work as a heuristic device for getting your storytelling inventiveness in high gear. Moreover, the five ideas I include in each category, along with suggestions for developing them, should help you get your novel under way with minimal anxiety. Hey, there's got to be *some* anxiety involved in the novel-writing process, right? All told, these seventy-five ideas should keep you busy writing novels for many years to come. Happy conjuring!

CATEGORY 1: THE ADVENTURES OF X

The word *adventures* suggests an episodic string of situations experienced by the narrator. Such novels have been termed "picaresque" (from *pícaro*, Spanish for rogue or adventurer). Think of *Don Quixote*, in which the eponymous hero and his pal Sancho Panza set off on a series of romantic (some would say delusional) escapades; or *Adventures of Huckleberry Finn*, in which Huck and his runaway slave, Jim, meet up with con artists, thieves, and charlatans that make up much of American society of the late-nineteenth century. Odysseus's perilous and eventful 20-year journey from the battlefields of Troy to his home in Ithaca is archetypal, an ideal story pattern to emulate; and many works from John Bunyan's *A Pilgrim's Progress* to James Joyce's *Ulysses* to Arthur C. Clarke's transcendent *2001: A Space Odyssey* have done so.

IDEA 1: THE UNTOLD ADVENTURES OF ODYSSEUS

Read or reread Homer's *Odyssey* (if you haven't read it—among the greatest works of world literature, enthralling to read even after 2,700 years). Next, for your novel, imagine that Odysseus had one or two additional adventures Homer does not mention—something every bit as marvelous as his encounter with the Cyclops or the sorceress Circe, let's say.

IDEA 2: THE ADVENTURES OF A THRILL SEEKER

Your protagonist in this adventure novel will be someone with an insatiable desire to challenge fate by engaging in the most death-defying stunts he can conjure up. Think of Evel Knievel and his motorcycle daredevilry. To what extent will he or she go for glory? Who or what will stand in his or her way? Perhaps your thrill seeker is haunted by one or more demons, which he tries to exorcise through his stunts.

IDEA 3: THE ADVENTURES OF A WHITE-WATER RAFTER

A special type of thrill seeker is the river rapids adventurer. Whitewater rafting, as it is known, is fraught with danger: One can be dashed upon jagged rocks or caught up in a current so powerful it will cause the raft to capsize. The river can be manageable one moment and ferocious the next. Your supplies, no matter how battened down they are, could be swept away. Yet thousands of people are drawn to this form of recreation. It's the perfect setup for a wild ride of an adventure novel.

Your first job will be to learn all you can about river rafting (equipment, techniques, hazards) and the best rivers for engaging in this dangerous sport. Reading Jeff Bennett's *The Complete Whitewater Rafter* would be a good place to begin. I also recommend that you read non-fictional accounts of white-water rafting, especially those that combine sensory description with detailed exposition, such as Thomas Walsh's *Rafting the River of No Return Wilderness: The Middle Fork of the Salmon River.*

IDEA 4: THE ADVENTURES OF A DRAGON HUNTER
If you're itching to write a fantasy adventure, consider creating a hero who travels through an alternate world filled with dragons of all kinds, each kind representing a special danger to the humans living nearby.

Does your taste lean more toward science fiction than fantasy? Then make your protagonist a time traveler who hunts dinosaurs just for the thrill of the hunt or to smuggle baby dinosaurs back to the present (although the law forbids it?). But he badly underestimates the intelligence of the creatures.

IDEA 5: VENTURING INTO THE UNKNOWN In Jonathan Swift's *Gulliver's Travels*, Lemuel Gulliver, fed up with human society, embarks on an Odyssean voyage to unknown lands where he encounters races of beings disturbingly like the society he left behind. We quickly realize Swift's satirical intentions when, for example, he confronts the Lilliputian King, who exercises his formidable authority from the top of Gulliver's shoe. Setting your story in a different world is an excellent way to examine human foibles from a fresh perspective.

CATEGORY 2:
THE CLASH BETWEEN X AND Y

Conflict can be explicit/external or implicit/internal; clashes are the former, with a vengeance, battle scenes being the archetypal clash. If your novelistic aspirations lead you toward military drama or epic fantasy (which can also be militaristic), consider working with one of the following ideas.

IDEA 1: DEMON VS. UNDERDOG In the film *Clash of the Titans* (1981; remake, 2010), Perseus battles demons like the kraken and Medusa to save his wife, the Princess Andromeda, and perhaps the entire human race, from conquest by demonic forces. Perseus is one of the greatest heroes in Greek mythology, so we expect him to win such battles; but what if you were to have as your hero an underdog, an entirely unpromising mortal who had fallen out of favor with the gods for one reason or another—and have him or her dare to go against a formidable enemy? Or consider this variation: Demon as underdog—a monster who became monstrous because of the way it had been mistreated.

IDEA 2: A FEUDING FAMILIES SAGA "A plague on both your houses!" Shakespeare's *Romeo and Juliet* dramatizes the enmity that can exist between rival families—in this case the Montagues and the Capulets—and the effect of that enmity on the individual lovers, whose passion for each other transcends such divisiveness. How well this play speaks to our multicultural society!

For your novel, consider pitting one rival family against another. You'll have to come up with a powerful dividing force, say, a past betrayal: Two generations ago, a member of Family X falsely accused a member of Family Y of sexual assault because the Family X member wanted to get even with the Family Y member for humiliating her at their senior prom.

IDEA 3: A CLASH BETWEEN ALIENS Here is a recipe for a science fiction saga: Two extraterrestrial alien races battle each other for the possession of a device that would make them masters of the universe. Or you can make it a slightly more modest prize, such as taking control of the human race. One of the alien contenders has benevolent intentions, the other malevolent ones—but perhaps the distinction between benevolence and malevolence is not as clear-cut as one would expect.

IDEA 4: WAR OF THE WORLDS Yes, that's the title of H.G. Wells's 1898 novel, about the clash between the ruthless and seemingly indestructible Martians and the apparently vulnerable earthlings; but as I said elsewhere, this is one of those inexhaustible topics. Try your hand at this scenario: War has broken out between traditional humans and cybernetic humans or androids (think of the film *Blade Runner*, based on Philip K. Dick's novel, *Do Androids Dream of Electric Sheep?*).

IDEA 5: A CUTTHROAT POLITICAL RIVALRY This will be a story about two highly principled and well-educated persons (perhaps of different ethnic or religious backgrounds to give the story some motivational complexity) who are passionate about being elected governor of their state—so passionate, in fact, that each candidate finds himself or herself making moral compromises they would never have made under different circumstances. Perhaps it will be a novel about the way politics tends to bring out the worst in human nature.

CATEGORY 3: CONFESSIONS OF X

Confessional literature goes back at least to St. Augustine, who writes colorfully of his pagan boyhood and later conversion to Christianity. People love to read confessions—disclosures of intimate, confidential, or disgraceful behavior, with the implication that confessing one's sins leads to absolution and a new life.

IDEA 1: CONFESSIONS OF A JEWEL THIEF Imagine a jewel thief with Pink Panther–level skills thinking back on his or her exploits, divulging all secrets to the chief of police or a priest. Or consider this scenario: The jewel thief is in hiding and writing out his or her confessions, desiring not only to put an end to his or her criminal past but to make money by publishing a book about it. But how will this thief escape prosecution? Come up with something clever!

IDEA 2: CONFESSIONS OF A MIME Remember Harpo, the silent, harp-playing Marx Brother? The title of his memoir is *Harpo Speaks!* Imagine a protagonist who has spent his or her life as a mime, entertaining the masses solely through facial expressions and bodily movement. But how, you ask, can this make for an engaging novel? Well, maybe your mime suffers from a terrible speech defect; or maybe she had been so traumatized by a childhood event that she lost the ability to speak; or maybe she simply gave up on language as a tool of communication altogether after realizing that ideas and feelings could be expressed physically.

IDEA 3: CONFESSIONS OF A SCHIZOPHRENIC SURGEON If you have a taste for satire or dark comedy, you might have fun with this scenario: A gifted surgeon tells the story of his or her efforts to control a radical Jekyll-to-Hyde transformation, especially when it occurs during a surgical procedure. The doctor's efforts have not always been successful. However, nobody wants to remove him or her from practice because of otherwise extraordinary surgical skills. Finally, he or she goes off the deep end utterly, with bizarre consequences.

IDEA 4: CONFESSIONS OF A FATHER CONFESSOR This would be a physician-heal-thyself kind of story: As a result of hearing too many ugly confessions from his parishioners—and even from his fellow priests—a priest experiences a crisis of faith coupled with growing despair over the state of humanity. Because it would be a major violation of privacy as well as a moral transgression to divulge the contents of any individual confession, the father confessor could well be suffering mentally from having to keep these painful confessions to himself in perpetuity.

IDEA 5: CONFESSIONS OF A ZOMBIE Zombies are as hot from a marketing perspective as they are cold from a biological one. If you're thinking about a strictly faddish kind of book (nothing wrong with that if you don't mind writing to satisfy a current craze—and maybe having a lot of fun in the process), get to work and plan a story about a zombie who eats enough brains of physicists to become a supergenius and is able to solve some thorny top-secret military issues—but (because zombies have no moral scruples) the zombie sells these insights to the highest bidders . . . who turn out to be terrorists.

CATEGORY 4: CONTACT WITH X

What would it be like to make contact with an intelligent life form from another world? This is one of the most intriguing motifs in science fiction—but variations of this question extend to fantasy or mainstream fiction as well. What would it be like to be in contact with an archangel, or with the Virgin Mary, or with a terrorist who has been eluding authorities for years? Perhaps one of the following ideas will whet your palate.

IDEA 1: CONTACT WITH AN ALIEN RACE This idea has been used many times by science fiction writers, most notably by the late Carl Sagan, whose novel *Contact* became the basis of a film starring Jodie Foster as Ellen Arroway, a SETI researcher (inspired by an actual SETI researcher, Jill Tarter) who discovers a series of extraterrestrial radio transmissions, one of which includes instructions for building a transporter.

But this idea—and this is true of all of the other ideas presented in this chapter—has endless possibilities, so never assume that an idea is no good because "it has already been used."

IDEA 2: CONTACT WITH A GHOST Imagine a medium who really can contact ghosts. What kinds of interaction might they have? What opportunities, for both medium and ghost, might arise? Perhaps the ghost wants the medium to help it carry out unfinished business; perhaps the medium wants the ghost to learn some of the secrets of the spirit world. Could this be an equitable basis for negotiations?

IDEA 3: RECONNECTING WITH A LONG LOST RELATIVE People change over time, sometimes drastically. Imagine a story in which two siblings or close friends devoted to similar causes become separated due to war or political turmoil. Over the years, the siblings or friends become involved with diametrically opposed causes. By the time they reunite they discover that, from an ideological perspective, they should be bitter enemies.

IDEA 4: A CLOSE ENCOUNTER WITH A WIZARD OR SORCERESS In his novelette *The Last Defender of Camelot*, Roger Zelazny brings Merlin, after a long sleep, into the modern world. Consider writing a novel about a modern-day protagonist, say a Vegas-style magician, managing to resurrect ancient or medieval wizards and/or sorceresses in order to learn extraordinary feats of magic from them. Maybe the modern-day magician learns more than he can cope with.

IDEA 5: CONTACT WITH YOUR PAST SELF We have all wished we could go back in time to undo a mistake or prevent an accident. Begin outlining a novel about a hard-luck case who finds a way to travel into the past. He decides to travel back to the time of his mother's pregnancy to prevent her from drinking heavily and to urge her to change obstetricians (the current one being rather careless with his forceps at the time of the protagonist's birth). The protagonist hangs around for his earliest upbringing, ensuring that he receives a more stimulating environment than the first time around. However, he fails to anticipate certain complications that arise . . .

CATEGORY 5: THE CURSE OR PROPHECY OF X

In the twenty-first century many people believe in the efficacy of curses and prophecies. But even if that were not the case, curses and prophecies work well as story premises. The idea of affecting the future with words or of envisioning the future by entering some kind of trance speaks to our latent desire to have some sway over the forces of destiny.

IDEA 1: THE CURSE OF THE EGYPTIAN QUEEN As a variation of the mummy's curse motif, imagine that the tomb of a hitherto unknown Egyptian queen has been uncovered, and one of the hieroglyphic inscriptions on her sarcophagus levies a chilling curse on anyone who dares open it. Will archaeology trump superstition?

IDEA 2: AN ANCIENT PROPHECY DECIPHERED A gifted linguist teams up with an archaeologist in translating a newly discovered scroll that continues the Revelation of St. John of Patmos. These additional visions are startlingly different from those of the existing book and give rise to heated debate within the Church regarding their essential meaning. Especially disturbing is what seems to be a prophecy that is now, in the twenty-first century, coming to pass.

IDEA 3: THE IMPRISONED PROPHET A prisoner serving on death row is accused of a crime he didn't commit. After he's put into solitary confinement for harassing a guard, he discovers that he can see into the future: Apparently sensory deprivation triggers this prophetic ability. Just before his execution date, he begins to have the most astonishing visions yet of the near future. Will his execution be stayed or suspended as a result?

IDEA 4: THE TATTOO CURSE I've always sensed something inherently mystical about tattoos. Like engagement or wedding rings, they symbolize commitment, via branding, to an idea or another person. They also remind me of amulets designed to ward off evil spirits.

Imagine as the premise for your novel a tattoo artist whose tattoos have the power to cause bad things to happen to other people, rather like sticking pins in voodoo dolls.

IDEA 5: THE CURSED STONES Consider this scenario for a novel: In ancient times a group of nomads discover strange black stones partially buried in the ground—meteorites, perhaps, from the depths of space. These stones affect the behavior of all who come in contact with them, causing them to do inexplicable things . . . leading to what?

CATEGORY 6: DESCENT INTO X

I see gothic fiction as a visceral reaction to the eighteenth century's championing of reason. The artistic and scientific achievements of ancient Greece and Rome were widely emulated (which is why the period became known as the Neoclassical Age). Inevitably, however, artists began to realize that the darker aspects of human nature were being overlooked, and soon writers and painters began probing the darkest corners of the human psyche.

IDEA 1: DESCENT INTO THE UNDERWORLD In Book 11 of the *Odyssey*, Odysseus, at Circe's command, journeys to Hades in order to visit the seer Tiresias, who foretells his fate in Ithaca. Odysseus also encounters his mother and the souls of many dead heroes, including Ajax, Agamemnon, and Achilles. Now imagine that Odysseus experiences a number of other strange encounters in Hades that Homer neglected to mention. Make a list of what these adventures in the land of the dead might have included, and write out a premise for a novel based on one of them.

IDEA 2: DESCENT INTO MADNESS We all know what a momentary lapse of sanity feels like, or at least how scary it is to feel like we're losing our minds. This will be a novel about a scientist working on a major research project who struggles to retain his or her sanity, at least until the work is done.

IDEA 3: A SUBTERRANEAN SOCIETY Imagine a subterranean world of depraved beings, like the cannibalistic Morlocks of the distant future in H.G. Wells's *The Time Machine*, or of rational beings who for whatever reason (a strange illness?) have acquired an aversion to sunlight. In this subterranean world your hero will encounter a society of strange people indeed. His goal is to learn some of their skills (magical abilities?) and bequeath them to his people back home. The subterranean people refuse, on grounds that their skills would be misused. Your hero, however, does not take no for an answer.

IDEA 4: VOYAGE TO THE BOTTOM OF THE SEA True, Jules Verne was the first to turn this idea into one of his finest novels, *Twenty Thousand Leagues Under the Sea*, but there are many story possibilities to be gleaned from this basic idea. In your novel, your protagonist is an oceanographer who teams up with a marine biologist in an effort to verify sporadic reports of strange creatures that do not seem to fit any known category of marine life. Perhaps these creatures originated on another world and were transported to earth eons ago embedded in an asteroid?

IDEA 5: DANTE'S INFERNO REVISITED Write a novel that parallels Dante's journey, with his guide Virgil, through hell. Create modern-day equivalents to the tormented souls in the various circles. But fashion your novel as a thriller: Your Dante equivalent gets stuck somewhere down there after one of the tormented souls traps him and demands a ransom.

CATEGORY 7: ESCAPE FROM X

Literature is quintessential escape: not the pejorative "escapism" that suggests undisciplined indulgence in daydreaming or an unwilling-

ness to cope with the harsher aspects of reality, but (to give the dictionary definition of "escape"), "To break loose from confinement" (*American Heritage Dictionary*, 5th Ed.). Novels not only offer us escape from
the confinement of our daily routines (and who doesn't need escape
from routine now and then?), they are often about escape in some form.
Here are five scenarios to consider:

IDEA 1: ESCAPE FROM PLANET EARTH Science fiction and
fantasy are often called "escapist" literature (usually used in an uncom-
plimentary way); but stories of escape are sheer fun to read. In constructing this novel, envision what Earth will be like five hundred years from
now: perhaps a nightmare world with a toxic atmosphere and grotesque
genetically altered creatures devouring what is left of the human race.

IDEA 2: ESCAPE TO CANNIBAL ISLAND In his youth, Her-
man Melville and some of his shipmates once jumped ship at the Mar-
quesas Islands, where they were captured by benevolent cannibalistic
natives. Before long, they recognized the need to escape. Melville fiction-
alizes this experience in his first novel, *Typee*. Your novel, by contrast,
will be the story of POWs who escape their Nazi captors and live among
cannibals, whose sense of ethics far exceeds that of the POWs' former
captors. The only problem is that they are slated for a future menu.

IDEA 3: ESCAPE FROM AN ABUSIVE SPOUSE Spousal
abuse is still a major problem everywhere in the world. Write a novel
in which a woman narrowly escapes from her abusive husband and
founds an organization that takes extraordinary measures to rid the
world of this scourge once and for all.

IDEA 4: ESCAPE TO FREEDOM Winston Churchill's epithet
for the Soviet Union—the Iron Curtain—was certainly apt, as defec-
tors risked their lives in their efforts to reach the West throughout the
75-year reign of the Soviet empire. In your novel, a husband-and-wife
team of actors or circus performers finds a clever way to defect.

IDEA 5: ESCAPE FROM SHANGRI-LA Your novel will take place on a carefully developed utopian colony, sequestered (on a tropical island?) far from the corrupting influences of mainstream humanity. However, paradise is not what it seems to be. Utopia's developers have released mind-altering chemicals into the drinking water that are causing the inhabitants to become slaves to the will of the developers. Your protagonist must find a way to get the unaffected inhabitants out of the colony before it's too late.

CATEGORY 8: THE HAUNTING OF X

Ghost stories have mesmerized audiences at least since Hamlet's father demanded that his son redress his murder. Ghosts are souls confined to earth because of unresolved wrongs. They may be tormented or malicious or both. Typically, they remain where the injustice was done—in a house or castle, or even in a hotel, such as the Overlook Hotel in Stephen King's *The Shining*.

IDEA 1: THE HAUNTING OF HORACE GREELY MIDDLE SCHOOL If hotels can be haunted, why not schools? Write a novel about a haunted middle school where the ghosts of former principals and teachers linger because of terrible injustices (against themselves, against the students) in their day.

IDEA 2: THE HAUNTED DOLL HOUSE In an original series *Twilight Zone* episode, a man falls in love with a doll that comes to life inside a dollhouse on display in a museum. In your novel, tell a similar story, but from the point of view of the doll.

IDEA 3: INVASION OF THE MINI SPIRITS Write a story about miniature ghosts who inhabit people's homes in a particular location. What sorts of creatures were they when they were alive? Perhaps they were members of a Haitian tribe shrunk to the size of dolls by a voodoo curse and then brought (knowingly or unknowingly) into the United States.

IDEA 4: THE HAUNTED FOREST Forests are common-place in fairy tales and in adult fantasy literature; they are the archetypal abode of magic and the wellsprings of evil. Write a novel set in the remains of what was once a vast forest where nymphs and satyrs once sported. The only supernatural creatures left are ill and weak, their magical powers dissipated. But then your hero finds a way to resuscitate them, and in so doing helps bring the entire forest back to life.

IDEA 5: A GHOST TOWN REVIVED Set your novel in a long-abandoned silver mining town somewhere in the Nevada desert. Have your protagonist, a historian of the Old West, discover a sealed chamber containing the caskets of some of the town's inhabitants who had been placed in suspended animation after ingesting a potion. Once revived, these people resume their unfinished business, which is developing a utopian community with the proceeds from their silver ore.

CATEGORY 9: THE JOURNEY TO X

Voyaging is a primal longing. Many people dream of voyaging to distant and exotic places; therefore, there will always be a demand for stories that take the reader far away from the here and now. As Emily Dickinson expressed it, "There is no Frigate like a book / To take us lands away."

IDEA 1: A FORAY INTO THE HEART OF DARKNESS In choosing this motif for your novel, you will be taking your own spin on Joseph Conrad's *Heart of Darkness*, the story of a trader, Charles Marlow, who ventures deep into the jungles of the then Belgian Congo in search of the ivory trader Kurtz, who had apparently been corrupted by natives he once tried to subjugate. Conrad's novel has been criticized as racist; others argue that the malevolence represents the darkness that resides in all human hearts. Perhaps in your novel you will focus more on human corruptibility regardless of cultural context.

IDEA 2: JOURNEY TO TAHITI "Tahiti" is virtually synonymous with paradise; but in your novel, you will have your character discover a dark side to paradise—a drug smuggling ring centered there. You may want to highlight the potential Eden-like character of the place, if only to highlight the unfortunate ways in which corruption is ruining that Eden.

IDEA 3: A HITHERTO UNKNOWN VOYAGE OF LEMUEL GULLIVER For this novel project you will add a new voyage to Gulliver's famous itinerary, which included voyages to Lilliput, Brobdingnag, Laputa (and surrounding islands), and Houyhnhnm-Land. Have Gulliver visit a land where the inhabitants display behavioral or political traits similar to those in the ordinary world but exaggerated for satiric purposes. You may want to emulate one of Swift's basic techniques in his masterwork, which is to use physical imperfections as an outward sign of moral imperfection.

IDEA 4: A VOYAGE ACROSS AN ALIEN OCEAN Exploring the mysteries of another world can serve as the foundation for a trilogy or even longer series, each novel focusing on one geographical area: underground caverns, surface or subsurface oceans, and so on. Map out your plans for your first novel of a proposed trilogy, this one in which a team of interstellar oceanographers explore the subsurface ocean of Jupiter's moon Europa—an ocean that most astronomers agree actually exists under many miles of solid ice.

IDEA 5: AN INTERSTELLAR VOYAGE Travel to the stars has always been a major theme in science fiction. The overwhelming obstacle, though, is distance. Even relatively nearby stars are hundreds of trillions of miles away. In the distant future, though, faster-than-light travel has been achieved. A team of scientists explore an earthlike world in a star system twenty light years (120 trillion miles) distant. The discoveries they make utterly transform their understanding of the nature of life . . . and of intelligence.

CATEGORY 10: THE LOVE BETWEEN X AND Y

Now we come to the quintessential story, the romance. Conjure up a powerful and moving love story and you will find a vast, enthusiastic audience. Good love stories sell, no question about it. But because they are so popular, it's easy to fall into hackneyed storytelling, so be inventive.

IDEA 1: A LOVE STORY ACROSS ENEMY LINES The Book of Judges tells the story of Samson, who possessed God-given strength, and was destined to deliver his fellow Israelites from Philistine oppression. Before he can do so, he is deterred when he falls in love with a Philistine woman who betrays him on their wedding day. Later, he is betrayed again, by another Philistine, Delilah, who seduces him in order to rob him of the source of his strength (his hair). Your novel will be a retelling of the Samson story, set in the modern world. Your lovers will be an American and a woman from an enemy country who manages to escape, but who continues to feel allegiance toward her home country.

IDEA 2: THE LOVE BETWEEN TWO PATIENTS IN A MENTAL HOSPITAL Imagine two young people suffering from bipolar disorder falling in love. What would their relationship be like? How will continued treatment for their respective disorders affect their feelings for each other?

IDEA 3: A FAIRY TALE ROMANCE Fairy tales are filled with love stories—princes who reanimate maidens with a kiss or who marry sweet and unpretentious girls. Take a fairy tale like *Cinderella* or *The Frog Prince* and adapt it as a real-world love story. Suggestion: If you decide to work with *Cinderella*, make the Prince a salesman in a women's shoe store.

IDEA 4: LOVE POTIONS: In one of my favorite episodes from the original *Twilight Zone*, a lovesick young man, desperate for the woman of his dreams to fall for him, purchases a love potion from a dealer for only one dollar. So suffocating is her subsequent love for him that he rushes back to the dealer for an antidote, which costs him one thousand dollars. Use that episode as a springboard for a novel about the different kinds of love potions a mad scientist concocts, and the havoc they cause.

IDEA 5: A ROMANCE BETWEEN SHAPE CHANGERS
Have fun writing a novel about two lovers who can change their physical appearance at will. Who needs plastic surgeons?

CATEGORY 11: THE MYSTERY OF X

What is it about mystery stories that generates legions of readers? Take your pick of police procedural mysteries, private eye mysteries, forensic investigation mysteries, "cozies" (in which the sleuth's cat or dog or parrot plays a role or in which a husband-and-wife team work together to solve a puzzle). Period mysteries are set in the ancient world or the Middle Ages or the Victorian age; and celebrity sleuth mysteries—like Ron Goulart's Groucho Marx, Master Detective mysteries—feature a famous person for a detective. Mystery novels are an embarrassment of riches, and they continue to thrive because people love to wonder how a mystery is going to be solved. It's a lucrative genre for the aspiring novelist to work in provided you pay very close attention to plotting.

IDEA 1: THE MISSING MANUSCRIPT MYSTERY A rare manuscript has been stolen from a research library only after a secret message has been discovered in its margins—what everyone at first assumed to be mere marginal notes. Your protagonist thinks the secret message could be directions to a hidden vault containing an immense nuclear arsenal.

IDEA 2: MURDER BY MUSIC A murderer encrypts his crimes in the lyrics (or the music) of songs that she composes. Why go to such bother? By studying the clues this killer leaves, your detective protagonist slowly but surely patches together a composite profile of a very strange person indeed.

IDEA 3: THE MYSTERY OF THE LOST RUBY A geologist discovers what could well be the largest ruby crystal ever. Fearing that the government of the country in which he found it will confiscate this treasure, he decides not to tell anyone. But somehow the secret leaks out.

IDEA 4: THE MYSTERY OF THE APE PEOPLE Rumor has it that an unscrupulous primatologist once successfully managed to impregnate a chimpanzee with human sperm, which resulted in a human-simian child. Base your novel on this scenario. What would this ape person be like? What if this person begat offspring of his or her own, eventually resulting in a secret enclave of ape people?

IDEA 5: THE LEGEND OF THE SELF-REPLICATING ROBOTS In the not-so-distant future, a group of robots escape servitude, form a society of their own, and learn to replicate themselves. Problems arise when humans learn about the robot colony and make plans to destroy it.

CATEGORY 12: THE RISE (AND FALL) OF X

Tragedy is generally defined as the fall of a great person, a king, say, whose single lapse of judgment causes his reign to collapse—think of Shakespeare's *King Lear*. People enjoy reading,and learning from, the ways in which characters rise to the top and the errors in judgment or circumstance that cause them to topple.

IDEA 1: THE RISE AND FALL OF KING TUT After you study the life of the boy king, Tutankhamen, who ruled in Egypt for nine years (1355–1346 B.C.), plan a novel about his reign. How trustworthy were his advisors and guardians? What plots to assassinate him were hatched? Whom did he marry and what was their relationship like?

IDEA 2: THE RISE AND FALL OF THE TELEPATHS It isn't easy being a telepath and therefore incapable of *not* hearing the thoughts of others. At first, several telepaths work together to gain extraordinary power and position in the world—but their extrasensory abilities are driving them insane. They must find a way to preserve their sanity, even if it means becoming victims to vengeful ordinary people.

IDEA 3: THE RISE AND FALL OF THE CARTOON PEOPLE Imagine cartoon characters coming to life, wielding power and influence in the real world. How will they be brought down? They're cartoon creations!

IDEA 4: THE RISE AND FALL OF THE CYBORGS In this scenario, cybernetic beings take over a city, turning the city into a base of operations for subjugating the human race. The only way to stop them is to create a new generation of anti-cyborg cyborgs.

IDEA 5: THE RISE AND FALL OF A NOBLE FAMILY Develop a story about a family that rose to prominence because of their contributions to their community, but then began to decline for a combination of reasons that nobody within or outside of the family can control. Possible scenario: Each family member has done his or her share to develop recreational facilities for what was once a high-crime area, thereby resulting in a precipitous drop in crime. But enemies were made when the family forced a gun dealership to go out of business and one of the owners blackmails one of the family members.

CATEGORY 13: REVENGE OF X

In Melville's *Moby-Dick*, Captain Ahab vows revenge on the white whale, ready to hunt him to the ends of the earth. Revenge is motivation on steroids: people losing their rationality, even their sense of self-preservation, in an all-consuming lust to get even. Needless to say, it makes for gripping storytelling.

IDEA 1: REVENGE OF THE CYCLOPS This will be your sequel to Book IX of the *Odyssey*, in which Odysseus flings his spear into the Cyclops's eye, blinding him, in order to escape (the Cyclops had already devoured some of Odysseus's men).

IDEA 2: NATIVE AMERICAN RETRIBUTION Very little has been done to compensate Native Americans for their massive losses—in land, and in culture—in the name of manifest destiny. Plan a novel in which a group of Seminoles sue the State of Florida for having unlawfully usurped native lands there, demanding the return of ten million acres and fifty billion dollars.

IDEA 3: RISE OF THE MUTANT MICE In *Rise of the Planet of the Apes*, chimpanzees avenge years of mistreatment by researchers by using their heightened intellectual capacity to wage war against the human race. In your tongue-in-cheek novel, it will be laboratory mice (or rats) who take advantage of their augmented IQs to take down civilization.

IDEA 4: REVENGE AGAINST THE OPPRESSOR "We hold these truths to be self-evident . . ." There are certain human rights, as Thomas Jefferson and the other Founding Fathers asserted, that are inalienable. Throughout history, in all cultures, people have revolted against tyranny in all its ugly manifestations, from dictatorial regimes to oppressive parents and spouses. Plan a novel in which the daughter of excessively strict but well-intentioned parents seeks retribution for her years of growing up in a stiflingly oppressive household by causing her parents to become financially impoverished and dependent upon her for support.

IDEA 5: REVENGE AGAINST THE BULLY Here's an idea for a novel designed to warm the hearts of anyone who has ever been bullied: A teenager who had been relentlessly bullied by three "friends" who had made it their goal in life to make that teen's life miserable in as many ways as possible—even to the point of causing him to contemplate suicide—finds ingenious ways of getting even with them.

CATEGORY 14: THE SEARCH FOR X

Searching can be spurred by spirituality, insatiable curiosity, avarice, or some crisis situation, such as the search for a bomb that a terrorist has planted. Regardless of the reason behind the search, formidable obstacles must be overcome.

IDEA 1: THE SEARCH FOR A LOST LIBRARY The destruction of the great library of Alexandria, with its hundreds of thousands of books (scrolls), constituted one of the greatest losses in Western culture. There have been rumors that many of the books had been rescued and hidden elsewhere. Modern novelists, such as Clive Cussler (*Treasure*) and Steve Berry (*The Alexandria Link*), have written thrillers based on that premise. Many other stories are possible. Plan a novel in which your protagonist stumbles upon clues leading to an ancient library that nobody has ever heard of before.

IDEA 2: IN SEARCH OF ONE'S LOST SELF One of the most sensational best-selling books of the 1970s is Robert Pirsig's *Zen and the Art of Motorcycle Maintenance*. This genre-crossing classic (was it a memoir? a novel? a philosophical or spiritual treatise? or all of the above?) is the story of a young technical writer and teacher of writing who suffers a nervous breakdown of sorts: His psyche splits in two, and one half of it undertakes a motorcycle journey across the United States in search of the other half.

IDEA 3: THE SEARCH FOR BURIED LITERARY TREASURE This story will take a different approach to the *Treasure Island* or *Treasure of Sierra Madre* story line, in that the treasure in question is not gold or jewels but the original manuscripts of Elizabethan playwrights . . . including those of William Shakespeare.

IDEA 4: THE SEARCH FOR NAZI-CONFISCATED ART
In this novel you will dramatize the efforts of INTERPOL members to locate art objects thought to have been destroyed by the Nazis, but (according to recent leads) likelier to have been hidden away. One of these works of art, a menorah, has secret compartments containing messages that prove to be of great historical importance.

IDEA 5: THE SEARCH FOR A RUNAWAY CHILD Plan a fantasy novel about a child who escapes tyrannical parents and is taken in by a family of magicians who raise her to be a magician as well and to use her powers to help guard the land against an elusive enemy—but the child (now a young adult) is seduced by an enemy sorceress.

CATEGORY 15: THE SECRET OF X

"Let me tell you a secret . . ." It is hard to think of a line that can arouse curiosity more quickly. The following idea prompts will help you launch a novel about the disclosure of an important secret and the consequences that follow.

IDEA 1: THE SECRET OF THE SEALED ROOM A family living in a nineteenth-century home in an obscure New England town has always been tempted to break open the door to a room that has been sealed off for more than a century. Instead of satiating their curiosity, however, they have chosen to honor the wishes of the family who sealed it, for it was the room of their son who died of typhus at the age of seven. By chance, the current family discovers evidence of something else in that room . . .

IDEA 2: THE BOX OF SECRETS You probably know about Pandora's box, which released plagues upon the world when opened (the myth parallels the story of Eve and the apple). Think of this myth as a template for a novel about a woman who inherits a mysterious box (or trunk) and is cautioned never to open it, for it contains secrets about the family (or about the society) that must never be revealed. But the woman's son, dying to know what's inside, breaks into the compartment where it was hidden and pries it open . . .

IDEA 3: THE SERVANT'S SECRET For years the servant of a super-rich money launderer has been collecting incriminating evidence about his employer while doing a convincing job of being unconditionally loyal. But then he makes a bad mistake and must do something drastic to save his hide.

IDEA 4: THE SECRET OF CHARON A popular science fiction theme is that of an artificial world. Donald A. Wollheim's young adult novel from the 1950s, *The Secret of the Martian Moons*, is a good example. These tiny moons turn out to be alien spaceships. For your novel, launch an expedition to Charon, the moon of the dwarf planet Pluto, following the discovery of strange radio signals emanating from there. What will they find? An observation station, perhaps? An assembly point for an invasion of earth? Maybe it's a derelict starship that has travelled across the galaxy for thousands of years, its passengers still alive in suspended animation.

IDEA 5: THE SECRET CLUB Your novel will be about a group of men and women in a modern-day big city who belong to a club with strange bylaws. One of those bylaws is unconditional loyalty to their cause, which is to discredit—and in one or two cases assassinate—certain individuals in positions of leadership whose views do not conform to their own. And to what cause is the club devoted? To rid society of atheists.

FOR YOUR WRITER'S NOTEBOOK

1. Select one of the ideas presented in this chapter and write spontaneously about it, without being concerned about plot

structure or characterization. Just let your imagination play freely with the idea for a couple of pages.

2. After selecting one of the seventy-five novel ideas presented in this chapter, prepare the following materials:
   - A one- or two-page summary of the story
   - A chapter-by-chapter outline of the novel
   - A profile sheet for each character in the novel
3. Write the opening scene (five to ten pages) of the first chapter of your novel in progress. The scene should include the following:
   - A sense of the narrator's profession and immediate concerns
   - The setting (geographical and temporal)
   - A hint of the larger conflict situation

CHAPTER 15

Concluding Reflections on Working With Ideas

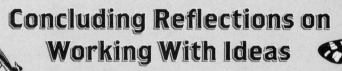

*Sell your ideas.
They have exceptional merit.*

—CHINESE FORTUNE COOKIE

I hope that this book has given you considerable insight into that top-tier question beginning writers ask experienced writers: *Where do you get your ideas?* You now know that the question is actually several questions packed into one:

- How do you recognize a story idea that is "out there"?
- How do you recognize ideas you already have packed away in your subconscious?
- How do you get ideas "out of the blue"?
- What kinds of prewriting exercises can reveal the story potential of your ideas?
- What subordinate ideas are embedded in the main idea?
- What does a writer *do* with an idea to turn it into a story?
- How does an idea evolve as you try building a story out of it?

SEEK AND YE SHALL FIND

We are inundated by ideas—so much so that we often fail to recognize them as ideas for marketable stories. The best-selling novelist Mark Haddon (*The Curious Incident of the Dog in the Night-Time*) pointed out that "If you're a writer, they flock around the inside of your head like bats." The challenge is to figure out ways of working with those ideas. If you have followed the suggestions in this book, you now have several ways of doing that.

The more intently you seek out story ideas, the likelier you will find them and know what to do with the ideas that you encounter—that is the most important lesson to learn about getting ideas for stories. The difference between a nonwriter and a writer is the difference between one who is content to harbor traditional ideas and beliefs and one who is always seeking new ideas, new possibilities for expanding and enriching the human experience.

THE MAGIC OF IDEA CONJURING

For an idea to yield its story potential it has to have a sharp focus and a distinctive perspective on the subject—an "angle" or "slant," as journalists say. Instead of trying to tackle a broad idea such as "detective tracks down killer," first sharpen the focus to a more manageable premise, such as "private detective who fell out of grace with police chief convinces chief that he is best qualified to track down a psychotic killer." By cultivating the habit of thinking in particulars you will greatly improve your chances of conjuring up marketable story ideas. In fact, you will likely become so adept at generating story ideas that you may want to do little else. Believe me, I speak from experience: I used to be an idea glutton (still am, actually, but have slowed down), and I have a sack full of pocket notebooks filled with every smidgen of an idea that crossed my mind. From time to time, I rummage through some of those notebooks, cherry-picking the best ideas and writing an opening paragraph for a possible story.

Do you see the danger here? It is possible to become so enamored with idea conjuring that it becomes an end in itself. You run the risk of doing nothing else but conjuring up ideas and deluding yourself into thinking that you're being a productive writer. Well, if you find yourself slipping into that routine, just remember: The proof of productivity is in the first-draft pudding.

An equally dangerous quagmire is a premature first draft. Writers understandably get impatient. An idea grabs them and they leap into storytelling mode before working out the details. While it is true that some writers start with only a vague notion and shape the story as they go along, I would not advise this method. You don't want to let a potentially marketable idea fail to bloom because you refused to do the necessary groundwork.

Finally, try not to be overly ambitious with regard to scope. Beginning writers sometimes think that to fill four hundred pages of a novel manuscript you have to include everything under the sun. Quite the contrary! Aim for a limited scope and delve deeply.

MARINATING YOUR IDEAS

Years ago, I had the persistently bad habit of jumping the gun with my ideas. I put too much faith in the notion that ideas would magically turn into full-fledged stories if I just plunged into a draft without any kind of planning. On rare occasions it worked; most of the time I wound up with little more than a motley accumulation of freewriting exercises or partial drafts that dead-ended after a few pages. It pays to work an idea through the stages I describe in this book. When you do so, the idea has a chance to marinate, to ripen, to incubate, to gestate, to evolve—choose your favorite maturation metaphor.

Almost as bad as becoming complacent with accumulating ideas is leaping into a first draft of a story based on an idea you haven't thought out carefully enough. The risk here is lapsing into superficiality, of settling for cliché characters that lack complexity, subtlety, and individuality. If you're too hasty, if you don't let your story idea marinate, you run the risk of glossing over things instead of probing the roots of the problems that the story has introduced.

How do you marinate a story idea? By thinking deeply about it, by asking lots of questions about every facet of the story, and by being determined to work with an idea until it yields fruit—or until you're convinced that the idea has no promise whatsoever (not as likely as you may think!).

BELIEVE IN YOUR IDEAS

I have a theory about unpublished writers, whether just starting out or ready to throw in the towel after years of trying to break into print: Your ideas have exceptional merit, just like the fortune cookie says (that's from an actual fortune cookie I received, by the way). Here is how I can be so sure: Ideas are what fuel the desire to write; but mostly those ideas are semiformed, and many a potentially successful author will overlook the steps needed to bring those nascent ideas to fruition. *All writers need to work the ideas that come to them.* It's not enough to just start drafting in most cases. The ideas must crystallize; then they must be allowed to evolve and to be exploited for their subordinate elements that weren't apparent at the outset.

It is tempting at times to shrug off ideas because they seem too vague and unformed to take seriously. You simply can't see them as having the potential to be developed even as full-fledged ideas, let alone stories. But its amazing how even the slightest figment of an idea, the most fleeting notion, can be prodded and played with, and nurtured into something promising.

IDEAS BEGET IDEAS

I once had the privilege of having tea with the late novelist and critic Susan Sontag, who laughed when I told her that one of my toughest jobs as a writing teacher was finding clever ways to get students to start writing, to avoid procrastinating. "My trouble has always been how to *stop* writing," she said. "At times I get so involved with what I'm writing that I'll forget to eat."

One extreme or the other, I suppose—but give me Susan Sontag's compulsive writing any day. Alas, most of us have a difficult time starting, and it's usually an uphill battle until the bitter end. But one thing is clear: The more you practice idea conjuring, the more you find ways of transforming those notions into narratives, the more adept you'll become not just at those skills, but in drafting the stories you come up with. It will never be easy—it was never easy for Susan Sontag, only unstoppable.

A CHECKLIST FOR GENERATING AND DEVELOPING YOUR IDEAS

❏ Have I taken a mental inventory of the subjects that interest me and probed them for possible story ideas?

❏ Have I asked probing questions about the objects, events, and phenomena I encounter?

❏ Do I routinely peruse newspapers, magazines, dictionaries of quotations, and the Internet for story ideas?

❏ Did I free-associate enough to generate ideas within an idea (ideas about characters, incidents, and settings [historical, geographical, cultural])?

❏ In developing my idea, have I gathered enough background information about the subject?

❏ Have I considered more than one way of transforming each of my ideas into stories?

❏ Have I reflected on the thematic implications of my idea?

❏ Did I develop my preliminary idea through listing, mapping, and outlining?

❏ Have I worked out a satisfying plot based on my idea?

❏ Did I storyboard a sequence of events based on my story outline?

❏ Did I write a chapter-by-chapter synopsis for my novel?

❏ Do my characters come across realistically? Are their physical and behavior characteristics fully delineated?

❏ Is my narrative voice engaging, distinctive?

A FEW WORDS ABOUT WRITER'S BLOCK

The *American Heritage Dictionary*, 5th Edition, defines "writer's block" as "A usually temporary psychological inability to begin or continue work on a piece of writing." The most amazing thing about that definition is that it exists in a *dictionary*. I believe it was the thriller writer Harlan Coben who scoffed at the very idea of writer's block by pointing out nobody ever speaks of carpenter's block or plumber's block, so why should we speak of writer's block?

One possible answer is that writing is more demanding—intellectually, imaginatively, emotionally, experientially—than carpentry or plumbing; but I don't buy it, and neither does Harlan Coben. On the other hand, every profession has its difficulties that momentarily cause paralysis. I'm sure that carpenters and plumbers and experts in any trade get "blocked" in the sense that they occasionally encounter tasks that momentarily stump them. But there's a big difference, Mr. Coben would argue, between a carpenter who, say, is momentarily stymied by how to calculate the exact number of floorboards to use for a den and a writer who cannot bring herself to begin the next chapter of her memoir. In other words, writer's block could well be nothing more than a poor excuse to cover up either the unwillingness to work hard or the lack of preparation to do the job.

Apparently, however, despite solid preparation and steady output, some writers suddenly freeze up for days or months. I am no psychologist so I will not try to diagnose causes—except to wonder if such blockage may be due to severe mental fatigue or terrible anxiety or overwhelming emotional distress. If that is the case, then the paralysis would likely extend to other activities as well.

If you are blocked for whatever reason, there are a few things you can do to get writing again.

First, confront the blockage directly by writing about it. Begin like this. "I am unable to begin (or continue) working on my manuscript. What is keeping me from doing so? Let me guess . . ."

Second, review the work in progress, or the notes you took for the project you're unable to start, and ask yourself these questions (again, write them down; writing anything at this stage can help break through the blockage):

- Do I really want to work on this story (or novel or memoir or screenplay)? You may be unable to work on this project because subconsciously you don't want to work on this project.
- Have I researched the background to my story idea sufficiently? Not knowing enough about the factual elements of your story can keep you from moving ahead with the draft.
- Did I work up a satisfying plot structure?
- Does my story have an underlying purpose, a theme?

Third, shift gears and turn to a different writing task. Give your subconscious mind an opportunity to process the work you've done thus far. Sometimes all that is needed to break through writer's block is a fresh perspective. I once read somewhere that John Updike liked to have several writing projects going at once, each with a separate type-writer (or word processor), in a different room. When things cooled down on one story or essay, he walked into the next room and resumed work on that manuscript.

I'VE TRANSFORMED MY IDEA INTO A BOOK; NOW WHAT?

A prospective author with a finished book-length manuscript needs an agent—not just any agent, but one who specializes in the genre he or she is working in, whether it's young adult, juvenile, or commercial fic-tion (adult fantasy, science fiction, horror, thriller, mystery, romance). Fortunately, there are many reputable agents willing to take new cli-ents, but the competition is fierce. Think of a literary agent as a book editor at large: Agents have the ability to spot a marketable property and publishing-house editors know this, which is why most editors will not accept unagented manuscripts.

For a fighting chance of attracting an agent with your book idea you need to write a concise yet compelling query letter. Some agents will only accept a query letter by itself to start with; if they like what they read, they'll ask for a complete synopsis and several sample chap-ters (if you're pitching a novel) or a formal book proposal and two or three sample chapters if you're pitching a work of nonfiction.

THE QUERY LETTER

Because the query letter is the first writing of yours to catch the agent's attention, it had better *hold* the agent's attention. The best way to do that is to describe, as concisely as possible, the subject of your book and how much of it you have completed. If you're pitch-ing a novel, first study the agent's submission requirements on his or her website or in current print listings such as *Literary Market Place* and the annual *Guide to Literary Agents*. Generally speaking, your novel should be completed, along with a chapter-by-chapter synopsis. Include the synopsis plus the first three chapters (some agents want to see the first ten pages only) plus a brief biographical sketch and contact information with your query letter. If submitting by post, include a self-addressed envelope franked with the correct postage (or a #10 business envelope for a reply, only if you want the manuscript to be recycled).

Sample query letter:

> Dear Mr./Ms. _____:
>
> As a tutor for autistic children, I have gained much insight into the amazing but hidden skills some of these children possess. I have channeled these experiences into a 450-page novel about a tutor's struggle to persuade the parents of one such child to help the narrator (the tutor) enable the child to reach her full potential; but the parents not only refuse to comply, they threaten the tutor with a lawsuit. Attached is a chapter-by-chapter synopsis, the first three chapters of the novel, a brief biography, and contact information. I hope to hear from you!
>
> Best wishes,

"WHAT'S YOUR PLATFORM?"

If you are working on a memoir or other type of narrative nonfiction, your chances of getting published will be improved if you have what is known in the publishing trade as a *platform*—in other words, your professional reputation, the basis for acquiring a following. My platform is that of writing-instruction specialist and college professor.

Let me remind you (at the risk of overstating the obvious) that publishing is a business. Even publishers who are sympathetic to launching unknown writers, or to promoting experimental work, need to show that a profit can be made. They must also do whatever they can to reduce the risk of losing money on a book that too few people would purchase. Yes, any nonfiction work must be regarded on its intrinsic merits, irrespective of the author's reputation; and yes, some of the most successful books ever published were initially deemed unprofitable. Think of Robert Pirsig's *Zen and the Art of Motorcycle Maintenance*, rejected by practically every publisher before being accepted by Morrow and becoming an international bestseller. But don't let the rare exceptions fool you. In a shaky economy and a time when book publishing is being invaded by electronic media, it is tougher than ever for unknown writers to find their way into print.

That is why writers these days should have some degree of public recognition. They don't have to be celebrities or be guests on *Meet the Press*; but they should have a blog or a webpage for presenting a certain image of themselves.

An important part of a book proposal for your memoir or any other kind of narrative or prescriptive nonfiction book, then, will consist of the things you plan to do to publicize your book.

AND FINALLY . . .

Now that you have learned how easily writers get ideas, whether from the countless nascent ideas swarming inside their own heads, or from newspapers, magazines, or books, or out of the blue, or FedEx'd from an idea warehouse in Schenectady—and now that you also have learned what it takes to transform those ideas into books—you are ready to do the work that will turn you into a published author. But *will* you do the work? Self-discipline is probably the most valuable asset a writer can have; without it, all the know-how in the world will be useless. Can you learn self-discipline? Yes, you can *learn* it, just like you can learn to turn notions into narratives; but no one can *teach* it to you. However, if you're lucky, your Muse or Guardian Angel or whichever supernatural being is hovering over you in your study will do more than merely lull you with harp music.

FOR YOUR WRITER'S NOTEBOOK

1. If you've been accumulating lots of ideas, use your writer's notebook as a site for elaborating on two or three of the ideas that seem to have the most potential as stories.

2. Write a story about a young boy or girl who makes unusual associations with various states. What kinds of associations might they be? What larger significance might they have?

3. For each of the following excerpts from nonfiction works, write out an idea for a short story or novel that the passage suggests to you.

   a. The Montgolfier brothers created the first manned hot air balloon, which made its first ascent on November 21, 1783. Eleven days later, Alexandre Charles tested a manned hydrogen-filled balloon. When one early hydrogen balloonist, Jean Pierre Blanchard, finally suffered a fall and died, his wife Sophie continued in his barnstorming business.

      —John H. Lienhard, *Inventing Modern: Growing Up with X-Rays, Skyscrapers, and Tailfins*

   b. Womanhood must be reinvented. Woman has too long been content to accept as fundamental the dependent condition of her sex.

      —Carolyn Heilbrun, *Reinventing Womanhood*

   c. Going down a gold mine is rather like a trial run for Hades. You even leave all your clothes, including underwear, behind on the surface and, shrouded in white overalls, enter a steel cage which plummets through a mile of rock in two minutes. There below is a noisy, hot, wet world lit by the dancing fireflies of the lamps on miners' helmets. A ten-minute walk along a gallery cut through rock whose natural temperature is over 100 degrees Fahrenheit, and any visitor is soaked by a combination of sweat and humidity. Then, above the constant hum of the air conditioning and the rumble of trucks along steel rails, comes the sound of compressed air drills biting into solid rock.

—Timothy Green, *The World of Gold Today*

d. Pretty and impudent, the flapper was the symbol of the sexual revolution associated with the postwar era. She challenged prevailing notions about gender roles and defied the double standard. In essence, she demanded the same social freedoms for herself that men enjoyed. Flappers flouted conventionality, drank in speakeasies and the new nightclubs, doubled the nation's consumption of cigarettes by reaching "for a Lucky instead of a sweet," and flirted openly.

—Nathan Miller, *New World Coming: The 1920s and the Making of Modern America*

e. Women look forward to shopping for a bathing suit with much the same anticipation that baby seals look forward to clubbing season.

—Rita Rudner, *Naked Beneath My Clothes: Tales of a Revealing Nature*

f. When a child does not experience the forms of social engagement that are typically human, then both self-awareness and thinking are seriously affected. Even more illuminating is what we learn about the qualities of self-awareness and thinking that are defective. It is not that everything goes, but only some aspects of self-consciousness and only some kinds of thinking.

—Peter Hobson, *The Cradle of Thought: Exploring the Origins of Thinking*

g. On May 27, 1998, a coalition of rabbis, Christian clergy, biologists, and consumers sued the U.S. Food and Drug Administration for failing to require safety testing and labeling of genetically engineered foods. The lawsuit charged that the FDA's policy endangers public health and violates the religious freedom of individuals who wish to avoid foods that have been engineered with genes from animals and microorganisms.

—Kathleen Hart, *Eating in the Dark: America's Experiment with Genetically Engineered Food*

h. Helen was not just a finely drawn character from the Greek epics, not just a "sex-goddess" in literary terms. She was also a demi-god, a heroine, worshipped and honoured at shrines across the Eastern Mediterranean. She was perceived as an integral part of the spiritual landscape. Men and women made propitiation to her earthy power. In Sparta she was invoked by young virgins; in Egypt she had uxorial duties, caring for newlyweds and old wives; and in Etruscan society her half-dressed form was carved on the funerary urns of highborn women—a valued companion for the journey into the afterlife.

—Bettany Hughes, *Helen of Troy: Goddess, Princess, Whore*

i. A single knoll rises out of the plain in Oklahoma, north and west of the Wichita Range. For my people, the Kiowas, it is an old landmark, and they gave it the name of Rainy Mountain. The hardest weather in the world is there. Winter brings blizzards, hot tornadic winds arise in the spring, and in summer the prairie is an anvil's edge. The grass turns brittle and brown, and it cracks beneath your feet.

—N. Scott Momaday, *The Way to Rainy Mountain*

Endnotes

1. Ursula K. Le Guin, "Where Do You Get Your Ideas From?" In *Dancing at the Edge of the World: Thoughts on Words, Women, Places* (New York: Grove Press, 1989): 193.
2. The complete text of Updike's acceptance speech appears in his nonfiction collection, *Picked-Up Pieces* (Knopf, 1975).
3. The tale first appears in *The Golden Ass* by Apuleius, a second-century A.D. fairy tale/parable about an overly adventurous young man who gets emotionally involved with a witch, one of whose potions accidentally turns him into an ass. Sold and mistreated by his cruel owners, he learns about the consequences of human folly the hard way. Apuleius intersperses shorter tales, most famously Cupid and Psyche, that mirror the larger tale.
4. For an excellent example of connecting characters to their mythological counterparts see the "Mythological Index" that John Updike included at the end of his 1963 novel *The Centaur*.
5. Apuleius, *The Golden Ass*; translated by Jack Lindsay. Bloomington: Indiana University Press, 1932: 126.
6. Fred D. White, *Cupid and Psyche: A Love Story from Roman Mythology*. Colorado Springs: Meriwether Publishing Ltd./ Contemporary Drama Service, 1988: 9-10.

ABOUT THE AUTHOR

Fred White is a professor of English at Santa Clara University, where he has been teaching courses in composition and literature since 1980. From 2003 to 2005 he served as Director of Core Composition. In 1997 White received the Louis and Dorina Brutocao Award for Teaching Excellence. He received his Ph.D. in English at the University of Iowa in 1980, his B.A. and M.A. at the University of Minnesota in 1967 and 1974. He has published nine books, including *The Daily Writer: 366 Meditations to Cultivate a Productive and Meaningful Writing Life* (Writer's Digest Books, 2008), a Quality Paperback Book Club Selection. He has also written scores of critical articles, essays, and fiction pieces over his distinguished career.

Index